ABC
of servicing and maintaining your Honda Unicorn

REGOS

First published in India 2012 by Wordizen Books
An imprint of Leadstart Publishing Pvt Ltd
1 Level, Trade Centre
Bandra Kurla Complex
Bandra (East) Mumbai 400 051 India
Telephone: +91-22-40700804
Fax: +91-22-40700800
Email: info@leadstartcorp.com
www.leadstartcorp.com / www.frogbooks.net

Sales Office:
Unit: 122 / Building B/2
First Floor, Near Wadala RTO
Wadala (East) Mumbai 400 037 India
Phone: +91-22-24046887

US Office:
Axis Corp, 7845 E Oakbrook Circle
Madison, WI 53717 USA

Copyright © REGOS

ISBN 978-93-81576-73-1

Books Editor: ParomitaUkil
Design Editor: Mishta Roy

Typeset in Book Antiqua
Printed at Repro India Ltd, Mumbai

Price — India: Rs 145; Elsewhere: US $6

To

> Parents – For not throwing us out,

> Friends – For madly cheering us,

> The bike – For letting us mess with it and

> The Late Sunil K Poolani of Leadstart Publishing –
> For noticing the worth in our work.

Declaration

Every attempt has been made to ensure that all the information in this book is accurate. However, no liability can be accepted by us or the publishers for any damage, injury or loss caused by following the information in this book or due to any inadvertent errors or omissions in the information provided.

About the Authors

The authors are childhood friends who share a lifelong passion for Motorcycles. They have spent countless hours fiddling with all kinds of motorcycles and hold a special interest in motorcycle design and maintenance. They both hold degrees in Mechanical Engineering and Motorsport Engineering and are budding First Generation Entrepreneurs.

Disgruntled over the years by the complete lack of information that would help a home mechanic (DIYer)/ regular bike owner like themselves, they have decided to put together a series of DIY style self-help books on motorcycle maintenance.

Contents

Preface

Bikes…

We own them,

We ride them,

We even love them.

But, how well do we know them?

We are a nation of Bikers. Every year, we buy close to 1 crore motorcycles. Bikes are not just a means of transport in India; they are a part of our lives. To the extent that some of us even pray for them…literally!

That said, how much do we know about our bikes? Ask yourself this question. If you are timidly saying "NOT MUCH" in answer, that's BRILLIANT. Yes, Really! That's the best starting point to learn, provided you have a bit of curiosity. We agree that every bike owner does not need to understand the intricate details of bike design. But surely we must all have faced situations where something goes wrong with our bikes, and we don't know what it is. We feel absolutely helpless. We can't be sure of what the problem is, let alone know how to fix it.

This helplessness and confusion exists at different levels in all of us bike owners, due to a general lack of knowledge. Also, there are several misconceptions about bike maintenance and servicing. To most of us, bike maintenance is washing and wiping it frequently. Bike maintenance is much more than that; it is a set of tasks that need to be carried out according to a schedule. Proper maintenance will keep your bike in best condition by enhancing its efficiency and performance and will also save you a lot of money on repairs. But the information about proper ways of performing the maintenance and servicing tasks is not readily available. This information is not just "Interesting-to-know" but "Absolutely Essential" information. It's your right to know about your bike and how to maintain it. After all, you have paid hard-earned cash to buy it.

We are very excited and proud to give you, India's First *Self-Help Guide to Motorcycle Servicing and Maintenance.*

The intention is to give an absolute beginner the insights into different components (Disassembly & Assembly) and their basic maintenance. Topics/ Chapters have been very carefully chosen and written in a very straightforward and simple manner. All the maintenance operations that can be done by you, at home, have been included. There are however, a few tasks that need to be performed occasionally, but are not described in great detail here. We chose to exclude such topics on Engine, Transmission (Gearbox) and suspension because, they require special tools and equipment, and are also beyond the scope of this book.

Performing the different operations explained in this book, will give you a lot of confidence and a reasonable amount of basic knowledge about your bike; and can also save money by avoiding frequent trips and tips to the mechanic.

As part of our research we had interviewed over a 1,000 Bike owners. We asked them several questions about what they knew about their bikes and how they maintained them. The answers ranged from shocking to interesting, but the most striking thing was the perception people have about maintaining their own bikes. Most of these people expressed very similar doubts about bike maintenance, so we tried to answer a few of them here.

Isn't motorcycle maintenance difficult?

No. Most of you must have seen very young kids working at roadside mechanic shops. Some of these kids are really brilliant. They can do all the servicing and most repairs on their own, without much supervision.

So the point is that, it is not difficult to service or maintain your bike. It is the lack of knowledge about the bike, about the tools and about the right way of doing things that make it look difficult. And that's the whole purpose of this book: to provide you with the knowledge about dissembling and assembling components, tools and the right methods.

Isn't it a specialist's job?

NO, it's not.

It would be a specialist's job if you wanted to service more than 10 bikes a day. Then, obviously, you will need lots of patience, practice and skill to complete servicing 10 bikes in 8 hrs.

But the case here is different. You do not have to be a skilled person to perform the basic maintenance tasks on your own bike over the weekend. This, by the way, won't take more than an hour or two.

Isn't it time taking?

'How often do you take your bike for servicing?'

In most of the cases it is once in 2-3 months. Next time when you drop your bike at a servicing centre, ask your mechanic how much time he would spend on your bike if it doesn't have any major repairing issues. We bet that you will be surprised by the answer.

We asked the same question during our research, and the answer we got was around 30-50 minutes.

So this should answer your question. Basic maintenance and servicing is not a time taking task. And you will agree with us once you start working on your bike.

Isn't it confusing?

When you don't know where to start and how to work, it seems confusing. Provided you have basic information and knowledge about what you are supposed to do, it will be fun and rewarding to work on your bike. And more over, when you perform the servicing and maintenance operations once, they become amazingly clear and easy. To believe us, you've got to try and get your hands dirty, at least once.

What if I damage something?

We have presented selected topics in this book and these operations don't need great skill. Each and every topic is presented with as many pictures as possible.

Moreover, no part of a bike is easily damageable, unless, you overdo something. The basic rule is that no operation on your bike requires Superman's strength, so if you feel that something doesn't fit with ease, the chances are that you are not doing it the right way. Always use the right amount of force required for the job, never overdo it. However, if you are not 100% sure about a task even by following the book properly, watch your mechanic perform the task once, and then attempt it on your bike.

Aren't the tools very expensive?

No, the basic tools (required to perform all the operations described in the book) are not very expensive. As per our survey, all the tools required to perform all the operations detailed in this book, would cost you less than 1,000 rupees.

We have carefully chosen the topics described in this book. And we have omitted the operations which require special tools and equipment.

Isn't my mechanic better than me?

Your mechanic is certainly better than you when there is a complex problem, like with the bike's engine, or when there's a serious repairing issue, his experience will be indispensable. But you are not likely to encounter these problems frequently, especially, if you maintain it properly and regularly.

Besides, when you are servicing and performing maintenance operations of your own bike, you will work out of love for your bike. Whereas, in case of the mechanic, it's just another day, another bike and another boring task.

Also when you perform these operations on your bike, you can be sure of your bike's condition. But when you trust someone else to do these things you cannot be 100% sure of the job.

My mechanic does everything needed when I give my bike for a service. Then why do I have to bother?

Surely you must have come across both good and bad mechanics. But, when you have knowledge about basic servicing and maintenance operations, you can at least choose a good mechanic, if you can't be bothered to work on your bike.

Introduction

How to use this book

Well, it's your book now and you can use it however you like. But if you ask us, to make the best out of it, we advise you to read this chapter first. It has some important stuff like Safety Guidelines and Servicing and Maintenance charts etc. If you have a basic idea about motorcycle maintenance, you can read any chapter individually, without necessarily following an order. However, if you are an absolute beginner, we recommend you to follow the books flow from one chapter to the other.

Also, before you attempt any task, we recommend you to read through all the steps involved first to get an idea of what you are going to do. Then start attempting it by following the instructions step by step.

Safety

It is quite disheartening to see page after page of safety instructions filled with hazard signs, warnings and crossed bones, when you are eager to start working on your bike. We understand this. But, as you will agree too, safety is indispensible.

However, we also believe that giving safety instructions like, "Don't touch your engine when it's hot, you could burn yourself" or "Petrol is highly flammable, working near naked flames can be dangerous" is preposterous. Not just because such things are blatantly obvious, but because it is nearly impossible to conceive or imagine all such possible hazards that might manifest while working on your bike. We are sure that our readers are well equipped with two of the most important prerequisites for safety: Common-sense and Presence of mind. So, we have listed out only those safety precautions and warnings which are not common knowledge.

Please take time and go through the following safety information before you start working on your bike.

Read all the steps involved in performing a particular task to understand the overall procedure involved, if you do not feel confident do not attempt.

1. We recommend you wear disposable gloves (latex or similar) while performing all operations.

2. Always make sure the bike's ignition is OFF before you perform any operation.

3. Make sure the bike is secure and steady on a flat surface. Your bike should always be on the main (centre) stand unless specified.

4. Work in a well ventilated place. Petrol and exhaust fumes are very dangerous especially in confined spaces.

5. Have a plan worked out for a possible fire accident. We advise you get a small fire extinguisher. A bucket of sand is a cheaper alternative (just make sure you don't use it to put out cigarettes or dumping rubbish). Never use water to put out fuel or electric fires.

6. Use non-flammable solvents like diesel for cleaning.

7. Brake pads and liners are made with materials that contain asbestos. So be very careful not to inhale brake dust.

8. Almost all the fluids in your bike like petrol, engine oil, brake fluid, battery electrolyte, etc. are harmful for your eyes and if swallowed. Prolonged contact with these substances can harm your skin too.

9. As a general rule, while trying to loosen stubborn nuts/ bolts using a spanner, it is advisable to pull the spanner towards you rather than push it. The reason simply is that, if you are pulling and if the spanner slips, you will fall on your bum. But if you were pushing, you would nose dive on to the bike and possibly knock off a few teeth.

10. Always replace your bike's parts with genuine Honda spare parts. Original spares are slightly expensive but for a good reason. Their parts are professionally designed and thoroughly tested not just for that individual part's performance, but also its interaction

with the other parts. Duplicate parts and spares can not only damage themselves but can damage your bike and can also risk your safety.

11. Always buy good quality tools. They might be slightly expensive, but they last longer and more importantly they won't damage your screw/bolt heads and nuts.

12. These are just a few generic guidelines. We have included necessary safety information where ever relevant within the chapters.

Tools

If your intention behind reading this book is to get a general idea about your bike's maintenance, then you won't need tools. By simply reading through you should be able to understand the different parts, their functions and their maintenance.

However, if you don't mind getting your hands dirty, and if you want to become a DIY (Do It Yourself) mechanic for your bike and do all the maintenance yourself, you will need some tools. We have listed all the tools needed to perform all the operations detailed in the book here. But don't run and buy all the tools now. Because good tools are like an investment, some prudence is essential. First decide the maintenance operations you are willing to perform on a regular basis. This will help you shortlist the required tools. Then as you go on you can keep adding tools as you need them. But if you are seriously considering servicing and maintaining the bike yourself, it is a good idea to buy all the tools.

Whether you buy some or all these tools, make sure you buy high quality tools. They will last forever and will also not damage your bike's components. Also, before you pay for the tools make sure you try them on your bike and check if they fit perfectly, because some tools (especially sockets and T spanners) might not be able to reach the bolts/nuts.

Screw Driver(s)	Med. Sized - Flat head & Phillips (star) head screwdrivers *or* a combination type screwdriver
Pliers	Hand/Cutting Pliers, Long nose Pliers
Hammer	Med. Sized Ordinary (0.5kg) hammer
Spanners	Open-Ended (ordinary)/Ring spanners of sizes: 8, 10, 12, 13, 14, 16, 19, 22, 31
	If you are not on a tight budget, you could buy combination type spanners. They are open ended on one side and ring type on the other.
	Also it's a good idea to buy both open ended and ring type spanners as kits. Up to size 22. And buy an individual spanner sized 31.
	T-Spanners of sizes: 8, 10, 19

Sockets	If you have deeper pockets, you could buy a Ratchet handle and a set of sockets. Also buy an extension that will let you use the ratchet like a T spanner. If you buy a full set of sockets and ratchet handle with extensions you could do away with regular spanners and T spanners.
Allen Keys	Allen keys of sizes: 6mm, 10mm
Slip Gauge	Unfortunately you can't buy individual slip gauges. They come in a bunch. So make sure you can measure 0.08mm, 0.12mm and 0.8mm.
Wire Gauge	You will need this to measure spark plug gap and also to adjust it. So buy one that looks and feels strong. It should be able to measure 0.8 - 0.9mm
Torque wrench	A torque wrench is a very good addition to your tool kit if you can afford it. It looks like a ratchet wrench, but it will tell you exactly by how much you have tightened a nut/bolt. It will make sure that you are not applying too much or too little force on any fastener. They come in different ranges and you will need one that can read up to **68Nm.** Also check if the torque wrench is compatible with the sockets you have. We have specified the recommended torque wherever applicable. This will give you an idea about the amount of force you need to apply while tightening a fastener.

Spray Bottle   You will need this to spray cleaning agents like diesel.

Bunch of Rags   To clean the bike and your hands.

Oil Tub   It should be shallow enough to fit under the bike's frame.

Disposable gloves   Buy a box of vinyl or any similar gloves. Make sure they fit snugly.

Servicing and Maintenance: At a glance

Service and maintenance tasks have to be performed periodically to improve your bike's condition and also to keep you safe while driving. The prescribed service and maintenance tasks and their schedules are given here in this chapter.

The different operations involved are sorted in to two sections: The ones in the first section can be performed by you with the help of this book. And the other section has operations that need to be performed at a service centre. When you give your bike at the service centre or a mechanic's, make sure you tell them what tasks you would like them to do.

Take a look at all the tasks listed below. You will notice that most of the servicing and maintenance tasks can be done by yourself with the help of this book. We advise you to have the book next to you while performing any operation given here. That way you can be sure of performing the tasks in the right order and the right way.

If your bike is new (pending its first free service or <1,000 km), it is very important to get your first servicing done within the specified time (Approximately after 1 month of purchase or by 1,000 km on the odometer).

WHEN TO DO	WHAT TO DO	HOW TO DO
Every 1,000 km	Lubricate the Chain.	Chapter 10.2
	Clutch Play check	Chapter 11.2.1
	Accelerator Play check	Chapter 11.2.2
	Rear Brake Play check	Chapter 9.2.2
	Check Chain Slackness	Chapter 10.2.1
	Check Idle Speed	Chapter 14.6
	Check Disk brake fluid level	Chapter 9.1.3
	General Lubrication	Chapter 2.5
Every 3,000 - 4,000 km	Clean Air Filter element (For non-viscous)	Chapter 4.2
	Change Engine Oil	Chapter 6.1.2
	Check Brake shoes and pads for wear	Chapters 9.1.3, 9.2.2
	Check operation of both brakes	Chapters 9.1.3, 9.2.2
	Clean and lubricate Chain	Chapter 10.2
	Replace Chain Link Lock	Chapter 10.1.2

	Check Distilled water level in the battery	Chapter **13**
	Clean Fuel strainer and screen	Chapters **3.1, 3.2**
	Clean Crank case breather	Chapter **12**
	Check Valve clearance	Chapter **7**
	Check Wheels and tyres	Chapter **8.2**
	Check Headlight Aim	Chapter **14.7**
	Check suspension for smooth operation	Chapter **14.5**
	Check and Clean Spark plug	Chapter **5.1, 5.2**
Every 7,000-8,000 km	Replace Spark Plug	Chapter **5.1**
Every 12,000-13,000km	Replace rubber dampers as a set	Chapter **8.1.2**
	Clean centrifugal oil filter	Chapter **6.1.4**
	Replace Air filter element	Chapter **4.1**
	Inspect and clean Air supply hoses	Chapter **12**
Every 20,000-25,000km	Replace Fuel Pipes	Chapter **12**

Reference: Honda Unicorn Workshop manual.

Maintenance tasks to be performed at the service centre

Every 15,000km	Lubricate Steering Stem Bearing
	Carburettor tuning
	Check torques on all nuts and bolts
	Replace Starter Clutch Bush kit
	Check and repack wheel bearings
Every 25,000km	Replace Valve Oil Seals
	De-carbonise cylinder head
	Change suspension oil
Every 30,000-35,000km	Change brake fluid

General Lubrication

Every mechanical system with moving parts needs to be lubricated. Lubrication not just helps the components move freely, but actually makes them more efficient and long lasting. Lubrication reduces friction, thus reducing wear and prevents rusting by protecting the metal from corrosive environment.

Practically every part in your bike which moves will need lubrication in some form or the other. The following table gives you all the information you need to properly and regularly lubricate your bike at regular intervals.

Component/ Location	Lubricant	When to lubricate(km)
Chain	Chain Oil/Chain Lube[1]	1,000
All pivot points[2]	Multipurpose grease[3]	3,000-4,000
Engine Oil	Honda Engine oil - 20W40	3,000-4,000
Speedometer Gear teeth	Multipurpose grease	Every time you remove the wheel.
Steering stem bearings (Let your mechanic do this)	Multipurpose grease	15,000
Lip area of any dust seal	Multipurpose grease	Every time you remove/replace it
Every O-ring	Engine oil	Every time you remove/replace it
Axle bolt surface	Multipurpose grease	Every time you remove/replace it
All bearing rotating areas	Multipurpose grease	Every time you remove/replace bearings
Wheel distance collars	Multipurpose grease	Every time you remove/replace them

Reference: Honda Unicorn Workshop manual.

It goes without saying that different lubricants have different characteristics and hence they cannot be used interchangeably or just about everywhere.

Chain Lube[1] – It is a custom made lubricant for chains. It generally comes in an aerosol can and can be a little expensive. However, it is very effective compared to the regular gear oil or engine oil.

Pivot points – Several parts of your bike rotate or oscillate around a fixed point. These points are called pivots. For example, your clutch lever pivots around a bolt, so does your side stand, brake pedal, kick rod, etc. So, walk around your bike and find all those pivot points and grease them.

Multipurpose Grease[3] – It's quite a popular lubricant and is easily available at a reasonable price. It is a good idea to clean the old greasy areas before you apply grease again.

WD40 – This is probably one of the most revolutionary products ever. WD40 is a multipurpose spray which has lubricating, degreasing, and anti-corrosive, water displacing and penetrating characteristics. It comes in a can and can be bought from most hardware stores. If cost is not a big issue for you, we recommend you buy a can.

Fuel supply system

The fuel supply system briefly consists of your fuel tank, the fuel strainer, fuel strainer screen, fuel hose, and the carburettor. Some suggest that the inlet-valve should also come under this list, but we chose to talk about valve maintenance (of both the valves) separately.

The names of fuel supply system components are self explanatory, so we shall not worry too much about briefing you about what they do. What we shall stress on however is the importance of maintaining these components.

The purpose of fuel supply system is to provide an uninterrupted supply of petrol to your engine and also make sure it is free from impurities. Petrol stations in our country are notorious for fuel adulteration, which causes most of the problems. There is however a problem with petrol itself. It "goes off" over time. To make petrol burn better, several additives are added to it. These settle down over time and form sludge. This stuff then blocks the free flow of fuel. So in order to keep the fuel supply system in perfect condition, you need to check the system for blocks, deposits and leaks.

In the following sections we shall discuss how each of these components has to be maintained. Fuel tanks are maintenance free except that they tend to gather rust over time. If you find rusty sediments in the fuel strainer screen, then you probably need to pay a visit to the service centre.

Removing/Refitting

Fuel tank

Spanner of size 12

Always be extremely cautious while handling the fuel tank. Petrol is volatile and can cause serious accidents.

1. The very first thing you need to do is to turn off the fuel knob (the ON-OFF-RES knob).

   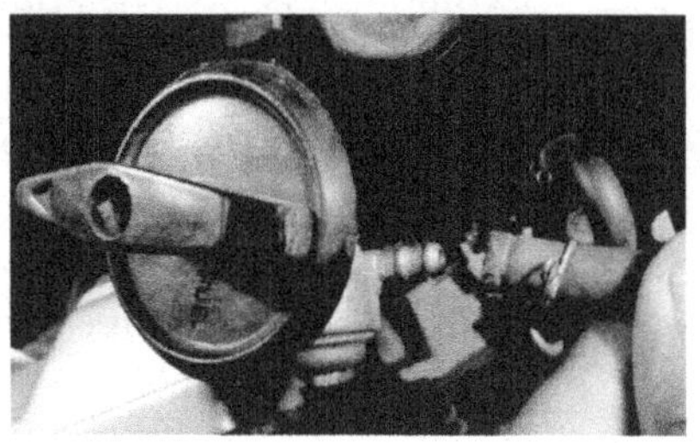

   Then pull the fuel hose (tube) that is connected to the fuel valve knob as shown in the picture.

   Note that your fuel knob might not look like the one in the picture here.

   Make sure the fuel is turned off and pull the tube out as shown in the picture.

2. Then, you need to remove the seat and side covers. Refer the respective sections to learn how to do these.

Once you remove the seat you will see that the tank is connected to the frame by a bolt at the position shown in the picture.

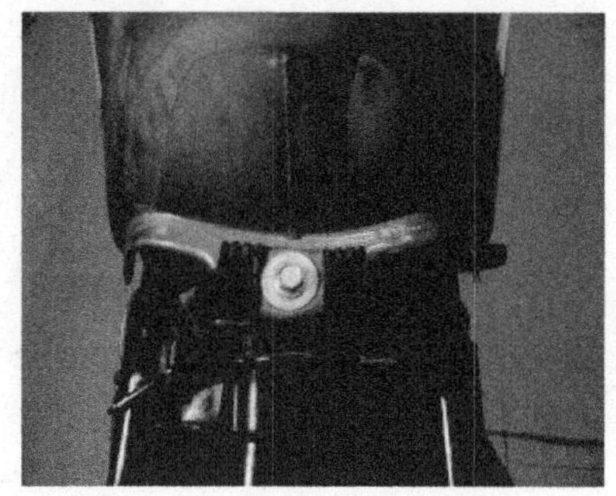

3. Unscrew the bolt with a spanner.

Pull the rubber cover back as shown in the picture to lift the tank.

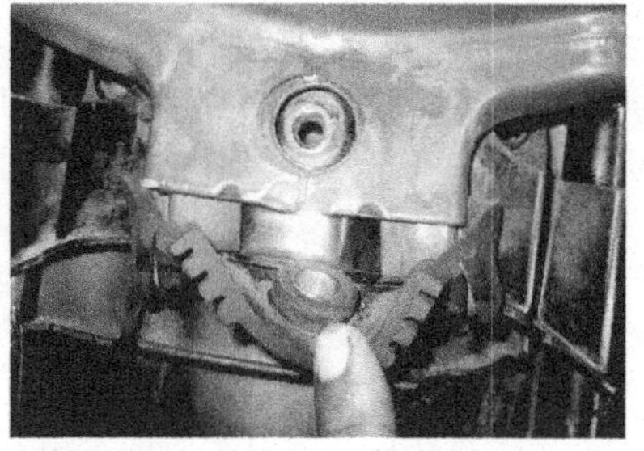

4. Now, hold the tank firmly with both hands and lift it up while tilting it slightly forward.

Don't lift the tank too high. It has a wire connected to it at the bottom. In the new model there are two hoses connected as well.

5. The wire connects the tank and the fuel indicator. There is a socket and plug joint, pointed out in the picture.

    This socket needs to be removed to separate the tank.

    If you are doing this for the first time and if the fuel tank is too heavy for you, you better call for help.

    If you are confident that you can hold the tank with one hand, gently remove the socket connection. Also pull the hoses out.

6. Observe the picture here.

    At the position where the fuel tank's front part sits on the bike's frame, you will find two round bushes as shown in the picture.

7. Take a look at the front end of the fuel tank. You will see that it has corresponding round braces as shown in the picture.

    When you replace the tank, you need to make sure that these braces slide on to the bushes.

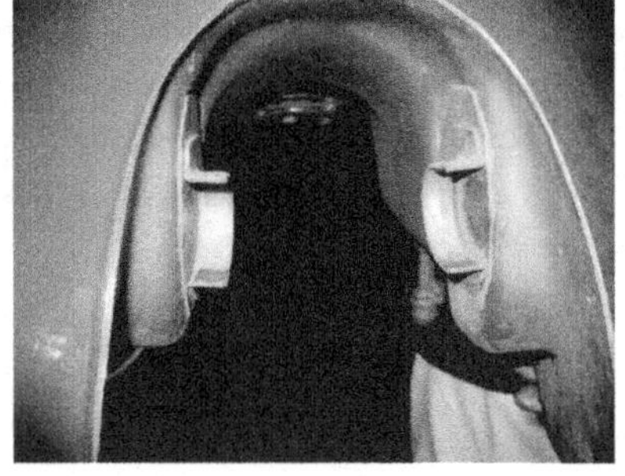

Fuel strainer and strainer screen

 Spanners of sizes 10 and 22

1. The first step is to drain the petrol while the tank is still on the bike.

   To do this, turn the fuel knob to OFF and get a clean bottle/container to collect petrol.

   Then take a look at the fuel pipe shown in the picture. It connects the fuel knob and the carburettor. Follow the pipe and find the point where its other end is connected to the carburettor.

   Simply pull it out from this end, stick it in a bottle and turn the fuel knob to ON. Petrol will start pouring out.

2. ·After draining the petrol completely, turn the fuel knob to OFF again.

   ·Then remove the tank and place it gently on the floor or work table.

3. ·The fuel strainer and the fuel valve assembly are highlighted in the picture.

    ·Also note the fuel strainer cap shown in the picture.

    ·Remove this cap using a spanner to access the fuel strainer screen.

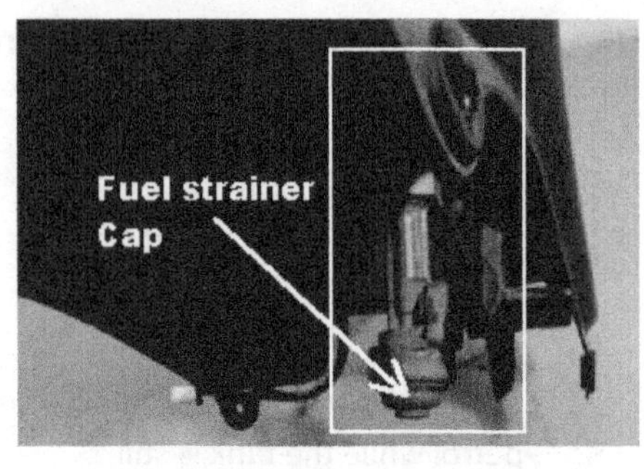

4. ·Once you remove the cap, you will be able to simply pull the strainer screen as shown in the picture.

    ·The strainer screen is just a mesh that separates any solid impurities in the fuel.

5. ·Then remove the strainer assembly from the tank by removing the nut shown in the picture.

6. ·Once the nut comes loose, you will be able to pull the strainer out of the tank as shown in the picture.

·That small tube is the strainer.

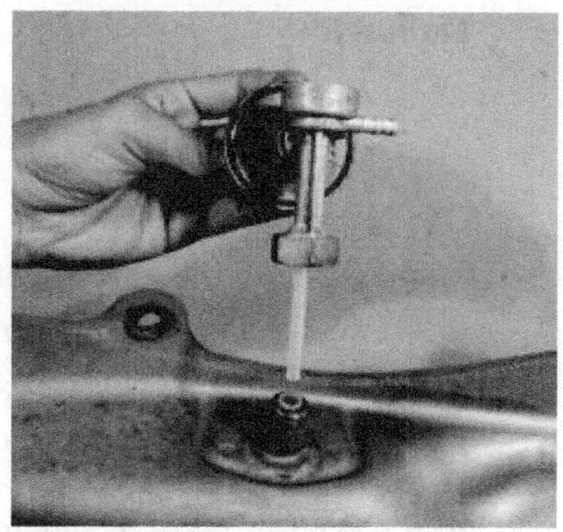

To refit the strainer and the screen, follow these instructions in reverse order. While refitting, check the condition of the O ring on fuel strainer cap, and if it looks damaged replace it with a new one.

Maintenance

The purpose of both the strainer and the screen is to filter any suspended impurities in the fuel. If they get blocked, the impurities will enter the carburettor and then the engine, which is bad. So it's advisable to clean these regularly. Simply follow the instructions in the previous section to remove them from the bike and then clean the parts using diesel and leave to air dry. Make sure they are not blocked and then refit them. Also, check if the fuel hose is cracked or blocked or has loose connections.

Carburettor

 A screw driver

To understand the purpose of the carburettor, you need to know how your bike's engine works. Your engine burns Air-Fuel (A/F) mixture and uses the power generated from the process to drive your bike.

In the A/F mixture, if the amount of petrol decreases, the power produced by the engine also reduces. If the amount of fuel in A/F mixture increases, the power generated also increases until a certain point. If the amount of fuel increases further, the efficiency of your engine actually falls and it also starts producing excess emissions. So, to make sure that your engine gets the right A/F mixture according to requirement, we need a device called Carburettor.

The carburettor gets air from the atmosphere through the air filter. It gets fuel from your fuel tank. It then mixes the right amount of fuel to the right amount of air and sends the mixture into your engine.

The carburettor in your bike is a CV (constant velocity)-type carburettor. It's noted for being very responsive and for improving fuel efficiency. It is also maintenance free.

It is also notoriously difficult to tune, so don't let the street mechanic open it and start blowing through the jets.

All you need to do to keep it in good condition is to drain

the float bowl whenever you are going to park your bike for more than 4-5 days. Petrol goes bad when it's left to stand for a few days. It will create deposits in the bowl.

So the next time when you are leaving your bike unused for a while, turn the fuel valve OFF and drain the fuel from the carburettor. To drain fuel from carburettor all you need to do is loosen the drain screw shown in the picture here. You will find it near the idle adjusting screw when you look at the carburettor from the kick rod side. Once the float bowl is emptied, tighten the drain screw **[Torque: 1.5Nm]** back.

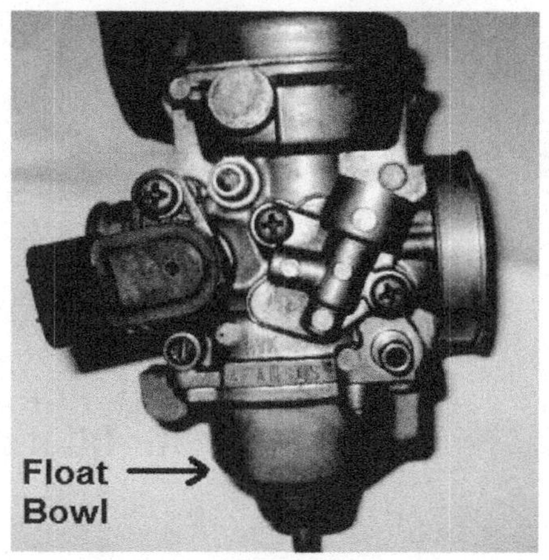

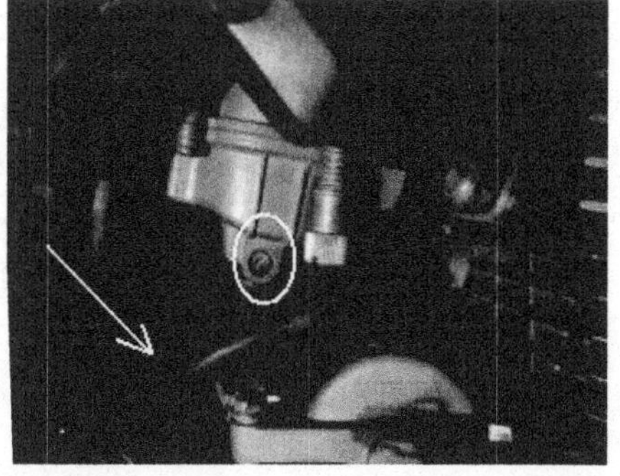

Air filter element

Your bike's engine cannot run on petrol alone. It needs oxygen (present in air) to burn the petrol. More than just oxygen, the engine needs air to create compression and for all the consequent steps. Obviously, it is also important that the air going into the engine is clean. The air around us has a lot of particulate matter, which can seriously damage the engine if it gets in. So we need a filter. This is called the air filter element, which is sort of a thick paper like material folded and attached to a plastic frame.

The first Honda Unicorn models (spoke wheels and kick-start type) had a dry-paper type air filter. The later models have a viscous (wet type) air filter. These are very similar, except that the viscous type ones have a coat of viscous (thick) liquid to help trap dust particles better. Both viscous and dry filters look alike but vary in colour. Dry ones are yellowish brown and viscous filters are green.

Removing/Refitting

Phillips Screwdriver

When you remove the air filter element, make sure dust or water doesn't get into the air filter housing. Preferably, cover it with a clean lint free cloth.

To remove the Air Filter element, you need to remove the seat first. Please see the Seat section if you don't know how to remove your seat.

1.   ·Once you remove the seat, you will be able to see the four screws pointed out in the picture near the fuel tank.

·The air filter element is under the rubber cover held in place by these screws.

·Unscrew all the four screws shown in the picture. You don't need to pull them out; you should be able to pull the cover along with the screws once you completely unscrew them.

2. ·Once you remove the rubber cover, you will be able to see the air filter element as shown in the picture.

3. ·You can remove the air filter by simply lifting it out as shown in the picture.

4. ·Once removed, it looks like the one shown in the picture here.

·To refit the air filter element, follow the above steps in reverse order. Do not worry about which side should face up/down, the filter fits only in one direction.

Maintenance

Compressed air or any air blower

Viscous air filters are maintenance free. So don't clean them. You need to replace them.

Viscous filters don't need cleaning they only need to be replaced every 12,000km; or a little early, if you drive regularly in abnormally dusty or rainy areas.

Non-viscous air filter elements need to be cleaned at every 3,000-4,000km and the importance of doing so cannot be overemphasised. Dirty air filters seriously affect the engine's performance and fuel efficiency because, they restrict free flow of air in to the engine and even slight filter damage can send all sorts of scary stuff into your engine and result in a nightmare. Also, because the air filter sucks in air from under your seat, don't put anything under there. The bike's papers, cloth, etc. should be placed only in the little compartment provided at the rear under your seat. Anything left out of the compartment will be promptly sucked in.

Hoping that we have scared you enough, let us see how the air filter needs to be cleaned.

To clean the filter, you need to blow compressed air along the folds (i.e. up and down with respect to the air filter's picture shown here) on both the sides.

You can use a small leaf blower or any such air blower to serve the purpose. You could even use a strong hair drier if you have one. If you can't get your hands on any of these, you should probably

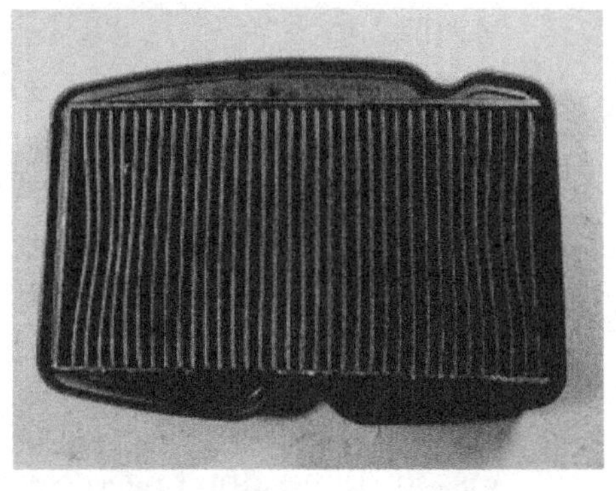

resort to tapping the filter against a wall or something to remove loose dirt and impurities. Because this is not very effective in cleaning the filter, you will have to do it more often; but make sure you don't damage the poor thing in the process.

When blowing air at the filter, always do so from a distance (3-4 inches) and at an angle so that the dust is driven out of the folds, away from you and not into your face.

If the filter looks too dirty, it's best you replace it with a new one. You need to replace the air-filter element every 12,000km anyway. And if your bike didn't come with a viscous filter, it is a good idea to replace it with viscous one.

Spark plug

The engine runs on air fuel mixture coming from the carburettor. This air fuel mixture is compressed in the engine by the piston and the compressed mixture is ignited by a spark from the Spark Plug in the combustion chamber.

When power is supplied from the magneto through a heavily insulated cable, it is passed to the spark plug through the spark plug cap. The terminal on the spark plug connects to the spark plug cap.

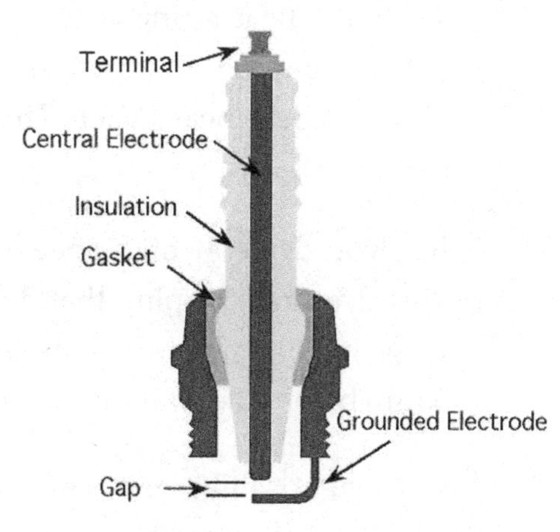

Source: Sparkplugs.com™

Current then passes through the central electrode and in order to complete the circuit, it "jumps" across the gap and then is grounded (through the engine block) via the grounded electrode.

This spark ignites the compressed air-fuel mixture in the combustion chamber. The resultant explosion pushes the piston down and thus rotating the crank shaft. This in turn rotates the drive sprocket via the gearbox. The chain then transmits this rotation to the rear sprocket and thus the rear wheel rotates.   The purpose of the insulator (shown in the figure above), which is made of ceramic (porcelain like) material, is to make sure the spark isn't generated anywhere inside the plug.

There are many types and makes of spark plugs in the market. Honda recommends NGK's CPR8EA-9 for regular driving, and if you are inclined to continuous high-speed driving, you might want to upgrade to CPR9EA-9. The numbers 8 and 9 in the spark plug code indicate the heat rating of the plug. 8 means the plug will take longer to dissipate (loose) heat and 9 means it will dissipate heat faster. These ratings range from 2-10.

When you drive at high speeds for extended periods of time, you need a plug that doesn't get very hot. If it gets too hot, the plug's heat itself can burn the Air/Fuel mixture before the spark is electrically triggered.

Because spark plugs work in extreme conditions, they need to be checked and cleaned during every service and ideally changed every 8,000km.

Removing/Refitting

Spark plug wrench or a spanner of size 16

·Before removing the plug, clean the area around the spark plug base to make sure that dust or anything else doesn't enter into the engine once you remove the spark plug.

·After removing the plug, make sure you stick clean lint-free cloth on the engine's spark plug-hole, so that dust or other foreign particles don't enter the combustion chamber while you are busy tinkering with the plug.

1. ·The spark plug is connected to the ignition coil through a heavily insulated ignition cable as shown in the picture. When you hit the kick-rod or push the start button, the ignition coil generates electricity which is transferred to the spark plug.

·And while the engine is running, current is supplied to the plug according to ignition timing so that the spark plug fires exactly at the right time.

2. · Before removing the plug, make sure your bike's ignition is switched off. If it's left on and if the self start button is accidentally pressed while you are working on your bike, you could get a massive shock.

· Then, to remove the spark plug, you need to remove the spark plug cap as shown in the picture.

· You just need to pull it out.

3. · Unscrew the spark plug using the spark plug wrench provided with your bike. If you have lost it, you can remove it by using a normal spanner of the right size. But make sure you don't damage the plug's hex nut.

· After unscrewing, pull the spark plug out.

4. · Installing the spark plug is a straight forward task. Before installing the spark plug, clean the area around the hole in which it sits.

· Also wipe the plug clean with a lint-free cloth and apply some grease to the threads

· Then, stick the plug in and tighten it **[Torque: 16Nm]** back.

· Install the spark plug cap.

Maintenance

Wire brush or toothbrush

Wire gauge

Maintaining spark plugs mainly involves cleaning them regularly and checking the gap between electrodes. Clean the plug using a lint-free cloth making sure you remove all the deposits. You can use a wire brush or a toothbrush to clean the threads and electrodes etc.

Then check the gap between the two electrodes. It should be between 0.8-0.9mm.Use a wire gauge or a feeler gauge to check the gap. Wire gauges are better because you can use them to adjust the gap too.

If the gap needs adjusting, do so gently. To reduce the gap, you can bend the earth electrode by applying slight pressure. If the gap needs to be increased, never do so by sticking a screwdriver between the two electrodes and "jimmying" them. The centre electrode is encased in an insulation which is quite brittle and will break if bent. If it breaks while the engine is running, the pieces will fall into the cylinder and damage the engine. To increase the gap you can use a wire gauge. Or hook a thin wire to the earth electrode and pull it gently.

Looking at the spark plug can give you a great deal of insight into how your engine and fuel system are operating. Take a look at the electrodes and insulator. If they are:

Brown, not oily and without much carbon deposit – Your engine is running in the right conditions.

White or greyish deposits – Too much oil is entering the engine. Consult a Honda service centre.

Wet oily deposits – Engine is badly worn. Needs immediate attention from a Honda service centre.

Dry, black, soot-like deposit – Too much petrol is entering the engine. Check your air filter for excessive dust or blocking. If that doesn't help, consult a Honda service centre.

Looking melted or almost fried – Ignition timing is set wrongly. Consult a Honda service centre.

Engine lubrication system

Your bike's engine has several moving components that continuously rub against each other. And hence, like in any machine component, you need to lubricate them to reduce friction and wear. This lubrication is taken care of by the engine lubrication system which comprises lubricant (engine oil), oil pump, centrifugal oil filter and oil strainer screen. Of the components, oil pump is maintenance free, so we shall not talk about it in detail here.

The lubricant (engine oil) plays an extremely important role in ensuring your engine's well being and extending its life and overall performance. Contrary to common understanding, the purpose of engine oil is not just to lubricate, but actually much more than that. It acts as a coolant, anti-corrosive agent and also suspends solid impurities like dirt and metal debris which are then filtered at the oil filter. So changing engine oil regularly is, without doubt, very important.

Honda recommends you to use **Honda Engine oil 20W40.**

The centrifugal filter and the strainer screen will need regular cleaning. As the oil keeps circulating to different components to both lubricate and also cool them down, it will gather a lot of impurities from different places and these particles need to be filtered to prevent damage to engine components. This filtering is done by a centrifugal filter and oil strainer screen. And those collected impurities need to be cleaned regularly to prevent blocking.

Maintenance

Engine Oil Level check

1. ·The first step is to put your bike on its centre stand. Make sure the bike is in neutral.

   ·Then, start the bike and let the engine idle for 3-4 minutes. This will warm up the oil and allow you to get the right oil level.

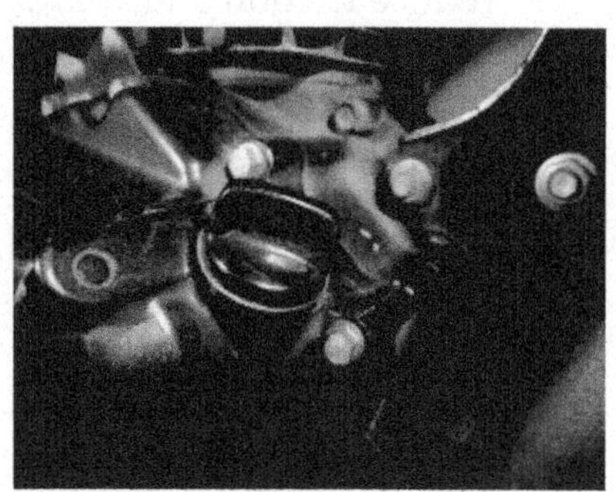

   ·Now, stop the engine and let it stand for a couple of minutes. Touch it carefully and make sure it isn't too hot.

   ·Clean the area around the oil filler cap to make sure dust or other particles do not enter the sump while removing the cap.

2. ·Remove the oil filler cap and wipe the dipstick dry with a lint-free cloth.

3. ·Insert the dipstick into the hole but do not screw it in. Simply dip it in.

4. ·Pull the dipstick out and inspect the oil level.

·The oil level should be between the Top and Bottom markings.

·If the level is between them, it means all is well.

·If it is just at the lower mark or below it, you need to top it up.

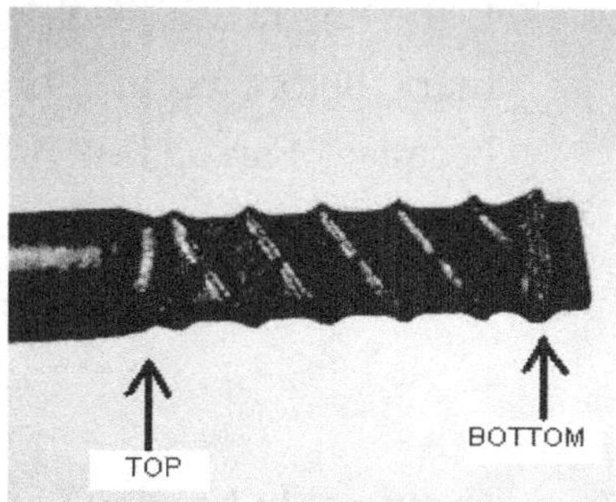

5. ·To top up the oil, stick a funnel in the hole as shown in the picture.

·Pour in a little engine oil, clean the dipstick and check the level again.

·Repeat the process until the oil level is between the upper and lower marks.

6. ·Take a look at the O ring (shown in the picture). If there is any visible damage, you need to replace it with a new one.

·Apply some fresh engine oil to the O-ring and then insert the dipstick and screw in the filler cap/dipstick.

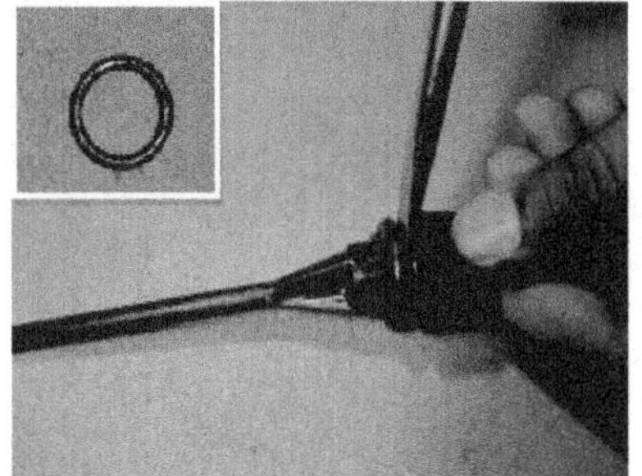

If the engine oil level falls frequently below the lower mark before regular oil change intervals, it could be because of an oil leak or faulty lubrication system. Take your bike to an authorised Honda service centre and have them check the problem.

Engine Oil Change

Engine oil needs to be changed regularly according to the specified schedule. If your bike is new (pending first service), you need to do your oil change much earlier, at around 1,000km on the odometer. This is because during the initial period before first service, which is called the run-in period, a lot of sludge and metal debris get deposited in the oil.

Spanner of size 12

Oil tub

Funnel

· Disposal of used engine oil is an environmental hazard. Whatever you do, do not dump it into the soil or flush it down the drain. Engine oil is extremely toxic.

· If you can, make an effort to give it to a mechanic who can recycle it.

1. ·The first step is to start your bike and leave it to warm up for 3-4 minutes, not more than that or you will burn yourself.

·Warming up will make the oil thinner (less viscous) and will allow it to flow out freely along with all the suspended particles.

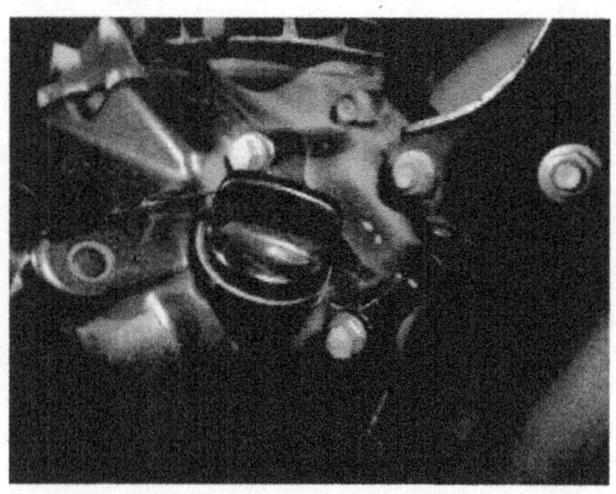

·Turn the bike off and let it stand for a couple of minutes. Touch it carefully and make sure it isn't too hot.

·Remove the oil filler cap and take care not to allow any foreign particles from entering the engine while you are busy draining the oil.

2. The oil needs to be drained from the bottom of your engine by removing the oil drain bolt.

The bolt is located at the point shown in the picture.

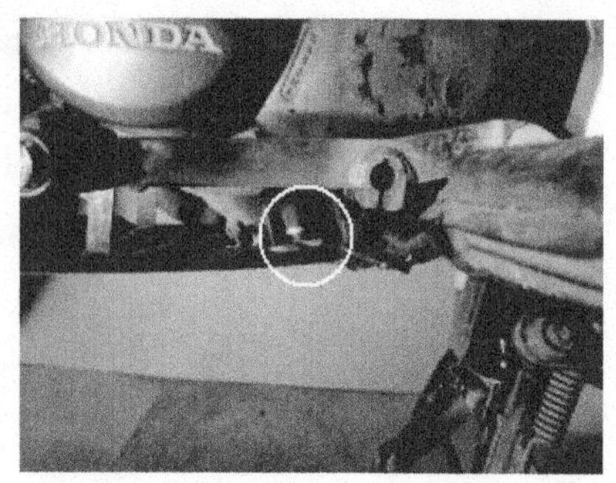

3 Get down on your knees and find the bolt shown in the picture (pointed out by the circle)

4. ·Now when you remove this nut, oil will start draining out from here. So place a tray under it first or you will make a mess.

·Using a spanner, remove this nut.

·As soon as you remove the nut, oil will start draining out.

5.

- The oil drain bolt has a sealing washer. The sealing washer is designed to deform under pressure so that it forms a perfect seal and prevents oil from leaking. So, this washer needs to be replaced every time you change oil or remove the oil drain bolt. So it's a good idea to buy a few of these washers.

- After the oil stops dripping, shake the bike a little to completely drain the oil.

- Apply a little fresh engine oil to the washer and threads of the bolt.

- Then fix the oil drain bolt along with the new sealing washer in place. [Torque: 30Nm]

- After fixing the drain bolt back on, fill up the engine with 1 litre of fresh oil.

Engine Oil Strainer Screen

Spanner of size 12

T Spanner of size 8

The engine oil strainer screen strains the oil as it circulates in the engine. It is basically a piece of metal mesh fitted in a small plastic frame. Its job is the same as the strainer filter you use at home to strain your tea. Only in this case, instead of tea it strains engine oil and instead of tea leaves it collects dirt and metal debris. It is important that you clean this screen periodically to prevent blocking.

1. · To remove the oil strainer screen, you need to remove the right crank case cover. To do that, you need to remove your kick rod first.

· Take a look at your bike's kick rod as shown in the picture.

· Note the bolt marked in the picture.

2. ·Remove this bolt using a spanner and pull it out.

3. ·Now pull out the kick rod slowly by holding it at the bottom.

·Once the kick rod is separated, the set-up looks like it is shown in the picture.

·Follow the steps in the reverse order to fit it back.

4. · The oil strainer screen should only be removed after you have drained the engine oil. Please see the Oil Change section to learn how it's done.

· After draining the engine oil, to remove the oil strainer screen, you will need to remove the right crank case cover shown in the picture.

· To remove the screen, remove the screws pointed out in the picture.

· Remove these bolts in two or three steps in a crisscross fashion.

5. · After removing the screws, pull the crank case cover off.

· You will note that the crank case and its cover have a gasket along their mating surface. It is a green (usually) coloured paper-like material.

· This gasket needs to be replaced with a new one when you refit the cover.

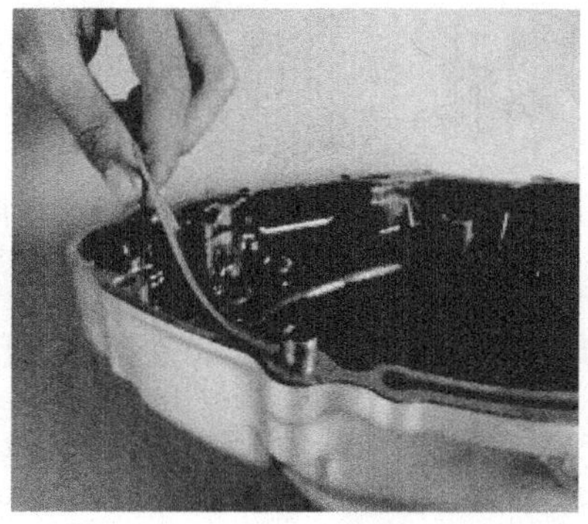

· You can remove it by simply peeling it off as shown in the picture.

6. ·After removing the cover, you will find the strainer screen seated in a slot as pointed out in the picture (bottom right, in a box).

7. ·To remove the screen, simply pull it out of the slot as shown in the picture.

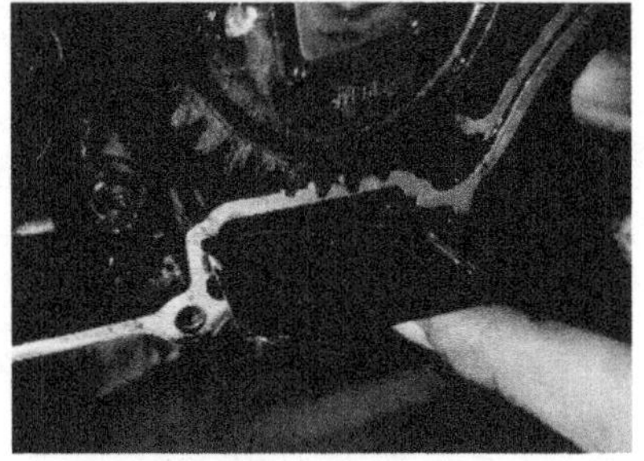

8. ·The screen looks like it is shown in the picture here.

   ·Any impurities in the oil get filtered as it flows through this fine mesh.

   ·To clean the filter of any accumulated junk, simply wash it off with diesel and leave it to dry. You could also use compressed air.

·To refit the screen, follow the above steps in the reverse order.

·Before refitting the crank case cover, install the new gasket by simply placing in position and then tightening the cover.

·Then make sure you have refitted the oil drain bolt. If you have, pour in the engine oil and refit the dipstick.

Engine Oil Centrifugal Filter

Spanner of size 12

T Spanner of size 8

Phillips screwdriver

The centrifugal oil filter, as the name suggests, uses centrifugal force to separate solid particles from the engine oil. Oil is fed into the filter which is then rotated at high speed. Due to the rotation force (centrifugal force), all the sediments are pushed out to the edge of the filter and the clean oil is re-circulated in the engine. These filters might seem primitive, but they do a pretty good job and together with the oil strainer screen, your oil is filtered very effectively.

However, if the filter is not cleaned periodically, it tends to build lots of dirt and gook. This can result in serious malfunctioning of the filter, at which point the sediments are repeatedly circulated in the engine leading to major problems even if the engine oil is changed regularly.

1. ·To gain access to the centrifugal filter, you need to open the right crank case cover. Please refer to the previous section to learn how it's done.

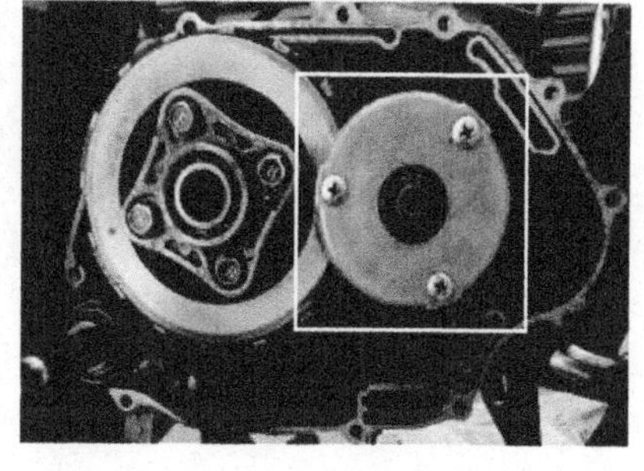

·After removing the cover, you will see a circular disk with three screws as pointed out in the picture.

·This is the centrifugal oil filter's cover. To remove the cover, remove the three screws using as Phillips screw driver.

2.

- Once you remove the cover, you will see the rotor surface along which the oil is rotated.

- Clean the rotor area with a clean lint-free cloth to remove all the dirt and oil. Make sure dirt doesn't enter the oil passage at the centre. Also, clean the cover. Note that the cover has a gasket (a green paper like material). Replace the old gasket with a new one if it looks damaged.

- If you are going to install a new gasket, clean the area where the gasket sits to remove any old gasket material stuck to the rim.

- Then, simply place the new gasket in place and refit the filter cover by tightening the screws **[Torque: 4Nm]**. Similarly replace the crank case gasket while refitting if it looks damaged.

- Finally refit the crank case cover and refill the drained engine oil.

Valve clearances

To understand what valve clearance means, you need to know what valves are and what they do.

As you may know your engine sucks in air/fuel mixture, burns it to produce power and then pushes out the burnt gasses. The engine head (the top portion of the engine) has two holes called ports, intake (inlet) port and exhaust

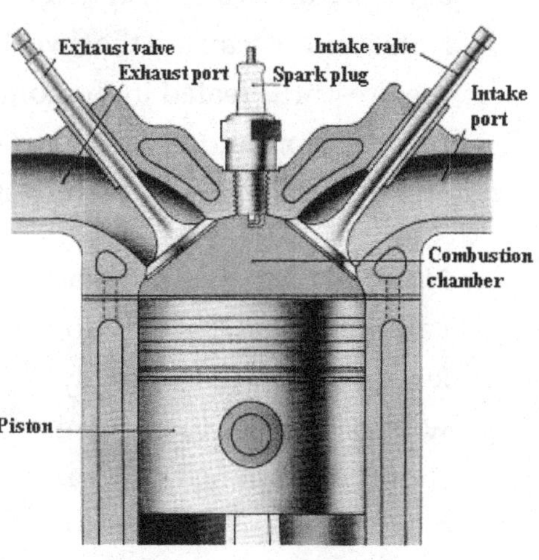

Source: www.etoyotaclub.net

port. The Air/Fuel mixture is sucked in from the Intake port and the burnt gasses are pushed out through the exhaust port. Bigger engines sometimes have 4 ports, two inlets and two exhaust ports. The purpose of valves is to shut these ports tightly at the right time to enable compression and also to prevent mixing of exhaust and Air/Fuel mixture.

Most automotive valves look like the one shown in the picture here. If you take a second look you will see that it looks something like a mushroom; that's why they are called mushroom valves or more commonly poppet valves. The valve head seals the port from inside out (i.e. the valve opens the port by

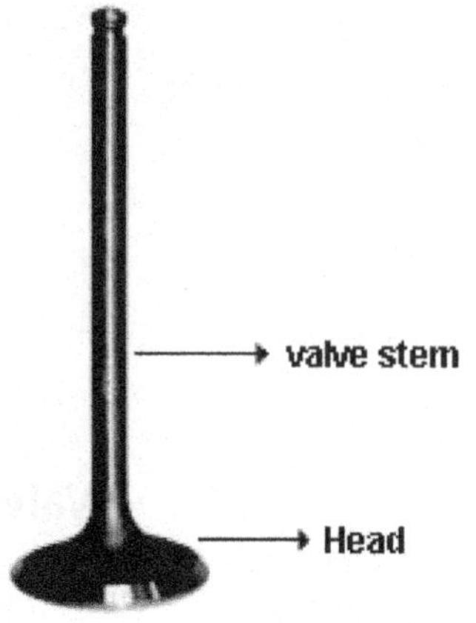

moving into the combustion chamber; see the picture above). Valves are designed to seal the ports by closing from inside because if they worked the other way around the pressure created in the combustion chamber during compression and combustion could lift the valves up and thus defeating their purpose.

Now that we know what valves are and what they do, let us see how they actually work. The picture here shows a simplified version of the valve mechanism. Cam shaft is a solid metal rod that rotates as the crank shaft rotates (crank shaft, by the way, rotates as the piston moves up and down). On the cam shaft there are little egg shaped protrusions called cams (as

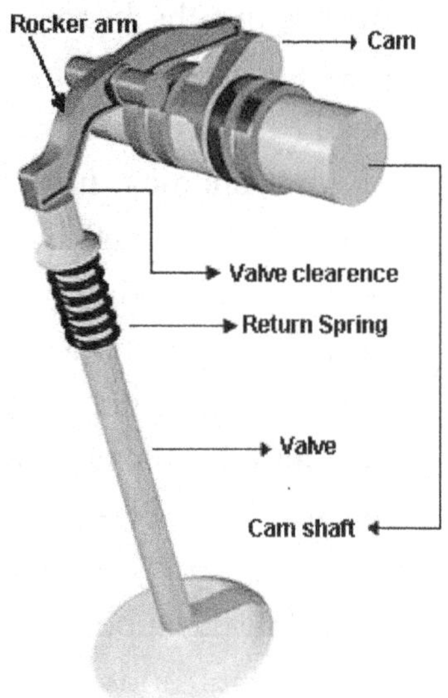

shown in the picture) which rotate with the cam shaft. As the cam rotates, the protrusion pushes the rocker arm (shown in the picture) up. And when the protrusion passes, the rocker arm will move down again.

So in effect, the rocker arm rocks (like a rocking chair, hence the name). By rocking, it pushes the valve stem downwards while compressing the return spring. The returning spring makes sure the valve is pulled back when the rocker lifts up again. Simply put: The cam shaft pushes the rocker arm which in turn pushes the valve into the combustion chamber (thus opening the port). And the return spring pulls the valve back and thus the port is closed again.

Looks like a lot is happening here, doesn't it?

Now dwell over this awesome fact: When your engine is simply idling i.e. when the engine speed is 1,000 rpm, each of your valves opens and shuts 500 times a minute i.e. around 8 times a second!

Valve clearance: There is a small gap between the rocker arm tip and the valve stem. This gap is called valve clearance (as shown in the picture above). This gap makes sure that there is enough space for the metal to expand and contract as the engine temperature rises and falls. Also, when the right gap is maintained, the valves will shut properly for the exact amount of time and will be able to dissipate their heat easily too. IF there is too much gap, the cam's protrusion keeps hammering the valve every time it needs to open which will obviously cause premature wear and damage.

Valve clearance keeps changing due to operating conditions and wear in different valve components. If this gap increases or decreases beyond acceptable limits, the precise time and duration of valve opening and closing will be altered drastically affecting the engine's efficiency and thus the fuel economy. It also results in additional stress and wear in the different components.

Hence valve clearances (on both exhaust and intake valves) need to be checked during every servicing schedule (3,000km-4,000km).

Valve clearance should be: **0.08mm** or **0.003 in** for **Intake valve 0.12mm** or **0.005in** for **Exhaust valve**

CHECKING VALVE CLEARENCE

Pliers

Spanners of sizes 10 and 8

Slip gauge

Allen keys of sizes 6mm and 10mm

Socket/T spanner of size 19

Valve clearance should be checked when the piston is in the topmost position (Top Dead Centre - TDC) in the compression stroke. This is when the valves are completely shut and also taken as a reference point to check clearance. Don't let the jargon scare you, it's easier than it seems.

Checking/adjusting valve clearance should be done when the engine is cold. Also make sure you have a new head packing/gasket handy. You will have to replace it in case it is damaged. And do not start the engine while doing these operations.

1. First, you need to remove the engine's head cover under which valves are located. To do this, you need to remove your tank. Please see the Tank section to see how it's done.

    Once the tank is removed, look at the engine from the gear shift pedal side. You will see the engine's head cover and the air supply hose (pointed out by circle to the right).

2. Disconnect the air supply hose by pressing the metal clips using pliers (or your fingers if you have super grip) and sliding the hose out.

3. Now remove the two head cover bolts pointed out in the picture.

4. Once you remove the two bolts, you should be able to simply lift the cover out.

You will see the cam chain, cam shaft and the rockers we have talked about in the Introduction.

5 Take a closer look from the top and you will find the two rocker arms as shown in the picture.

Note the point highlighted by the circle to the right. This is where the rocker arm actually pushes the vales in.

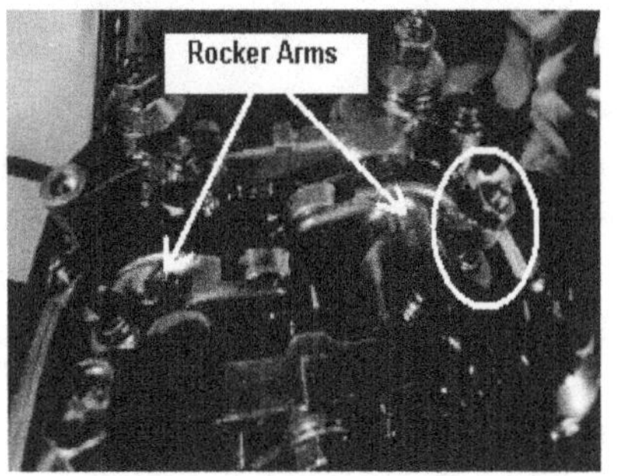

The valve on the exhaust pipe side is the exhaust valve and the valve on the carburettor side is the inlet valve.

6   Here is a close-up picture of the area pointed out by the circle above.

S = **Return spring** (The valve stem is inside this spring)
R = **Rocker arm body**
L= **Lock nut**
A = **Adjusting screw**
VC = **Valve Clearance** (Please refer the next picture for a closer view)

By tightening/loosening the adjusting screw **A**, you can decrease/increase the valve clearance.

The purpose of lock nut **L** is to lock the adjusting screw after the desired valve clearance is achieved.

7   The picture here is an extreme close-up of the valve clearance. Understandably, a gap of 0.08/0.12mm is little hard to see. But, we hope it gives you an idea about the precise engineering involved in your engine.

This is the gap (clearance) that needs to be checked/adjusted.

8   Next step is to remove the
  1.   Timing Hole cap and
  2.   Crankshaft hole cap using Allen keys.

Through the Crankshaft Hole cap, you can insert a size 19 socket and rotate the crankshaft. This will make your piston go up and down.

9   As said above, by rotating the crankshaft, you will be making the piston go up and down. By doing this we need to find the crankshaft position where the piston shall be in the topmost position.

In order to find out when it has reached the topmost point (**TDC**), there is a small provision called the Timing hole. While rotating the crankshaft, look through the Timing Hole.

Through this hole you will see the flywheel rotating (a portion of it actually). On the fly wheel, there is a "T" mark engraved.

You need to rotate the crankshaft until this T mark coincides with the notch shown in the picture. At this position, the piston will be in TDC.

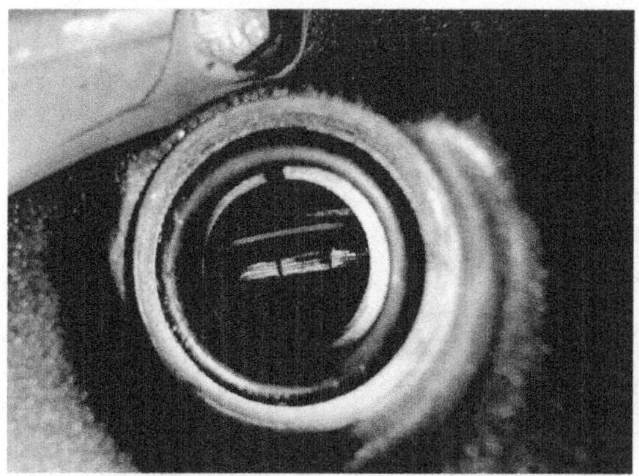

Now, hold one of the rocker arms and try moving it up and down. It will only move a little. If it does, your piston is in TDC during compression.

If it doesn't move at all, it means the piston is at the TDC during exhaust stroke. At this point the exhaust valve will be open, which is of no use to us.

In such case, rotate the crankshaft for one full rotation and match the "T" marking with the notch again. Check if the rocker arm moves. If it does this time, you are all set.

10 Now, get your slip gauge and find the blade of appropriate size. (0.08mm - inlet & 0.12 – exhaust)

Then, slide it through the gap shown in step 7. It should just fit through this gap. If the gap is too big, loosen the lock nut and tighten the adjusting nut using your hand and check the clearance again.

Once the gap is just enough to stick the slip gauge, it is good.

Now holding the adjusting screw in that position, tighten the locknut **[Torque: 1.5Nm]**.

Checking and adjusting valve clearance is the same for both valves.

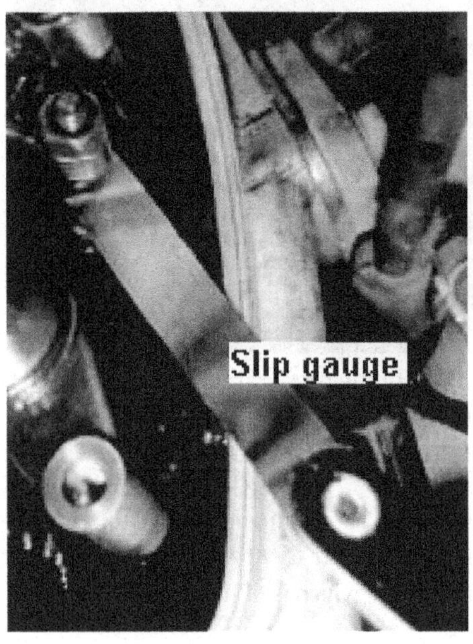

Refitting:

Once you have checked/adjusted the valve clearance on both the valves, you can go ahead and refit the engine head cover by tightening the cover bolts **[Torque: 10Nm]**.

But make sure you check the condition of the cover packing/gasket (the rubber thing). If it looks worn or damaged, replace it with a new one.

Replace the Timing Hole cap **[Torque: 10Nm]** and Crankshaft Hole cap **[Torque: 15Nm]**. While replacing them back keep an eye on their O rings. If they look visibly damaged, you need to replace them.

Wheels

Wheels need to be removed for performing various servicing and maintenance operations like brakes etc. It also helps in case you have a flat tyre (while you are at home obviously). You can simply carry the wheel to get it fixed instead of pushing the bike and half-kill yourself.

Removing/Refitting

Front wheel

Spanner of size 19

A hammer

Screwdriver

When the front wheel is removed, remember that you should not press the brake lever at all until you have finished refitting. Because when the wheel is removed, the disk won't be there to stop the pads from coming in to contact if brake is applied. If they do press against each other, it takes a lot of effort to prise them apart to refit the wheel.

1. ·Before removing the wheels make sure you park the bike on its centre stand.

   ·Place a box or something similar under the bike near the centre stand. This box will prevent the bike from falling over to the front.

·When you remove the front wheel, the bike's weight will shift backward and will naturally be stable. But it's advisable to have a backup.

·Make sure that the box supports the bike's frame but not the crank case.

2. ·Disconnect the speedometer cable as explained in the Cables chapter by pushing the cable tab using a screwdriver as shown in the picture.

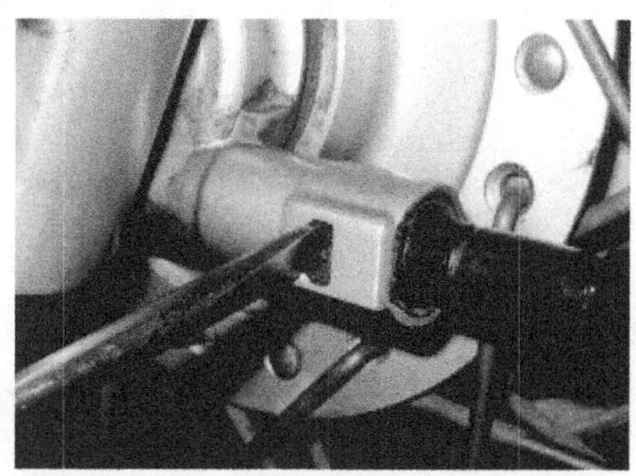

3. ·Then, using a spanner, remove the axle nut as shown in the picture.

4. ·After you remove the axle nut like in the picture, you will see the axle bolt. Hit this axle bolt gently with a hammer.

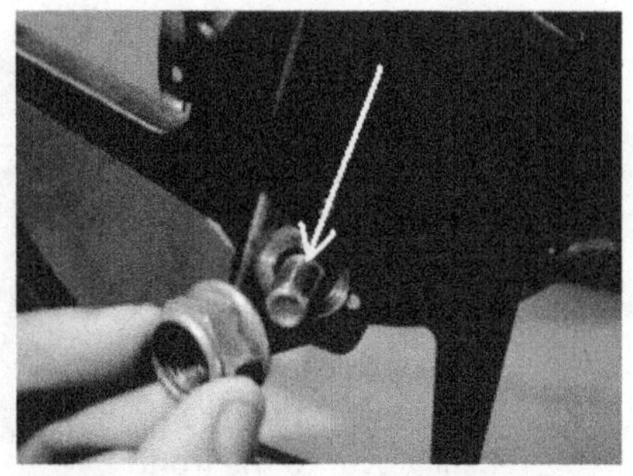

5. Then, go to the other side of the wheel and pull out the axle bolt while holding the wheel with the other hand.

6. ·When you pull the bolt out, the wheel will become free as shown in the picture.

·Now you can take out the wheel by gently pulling it from under the mudguard (fender).

·Once the wheel is out, make sure you don't drop it on the disk brake side.

·Disks can get bent easily on impact and bent disks are very dangerous to drive with. So be cautious.

·Make it lean against a wall.

·Also, make sure no one presses the front brake lever while the wheel is off. Because the disk is no longer in between the pads, they will press against each other and it will be hard to prise them apart.

7.   ·Next, remove the speedometer gear box by simply pulling it out as shown in the picture.

8.   · Now, take a look at the other side of the wheel.

·At the centre, in the hole, you will see that there is a metal bush as shown in the picture called the side collar. Pull it out as shown in the picture.

· The side collar can simply fall off the wheel when you pull the axle bolt out. So be careful not to lose it.

To refit the front wheel, follow the above steps in the reverse order. However, make sure you take care of the following points as you proceed.

1. ·Note that the speedometer gearbox has two notches as shown in the picture.

Also, one of the front fork's legs has a boss (protrusion) as shown in the picture.

2. ·While refitting the wheel, make sure that the boss on the fork leg sits between the two notches as shown in the picture.

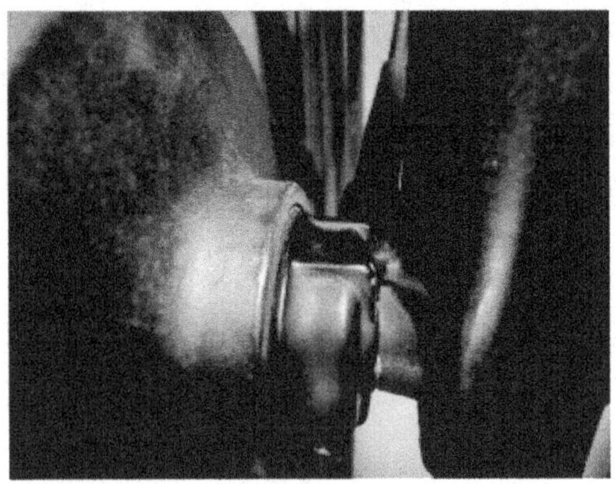

3. ·Apply a thin layer of Multipurpose grease on the axle before you install it.

·Also, apply some grease on the inner surface of the sleeve.

·When you put the wheel back on, make sure you put the collar properly in place as shown in the picture.

·Tighten the axle bolt **[Torque: 59Nm]**.

Rear wheel

Spanners of sizes 22, 14, 13

Hammer

1. ·Before removing the rear wheel, park your bike on its centre stand.

·Place a box or something similar under the bike near the centre stand. This will prevent the bike from toppling once you remove the wheel.

·Make sure that the box supports the bike's frame but not the crank case.

·Take a look at your rear wheel from under the silencer.
·   You will see the components shown in the picture.

- **A**=axle nut
- **B**=brake adjusting nut
- **C**=stopper arm nut
- **P**=adjusting plate

·   Remove all three nuts, A, B and C shown below.

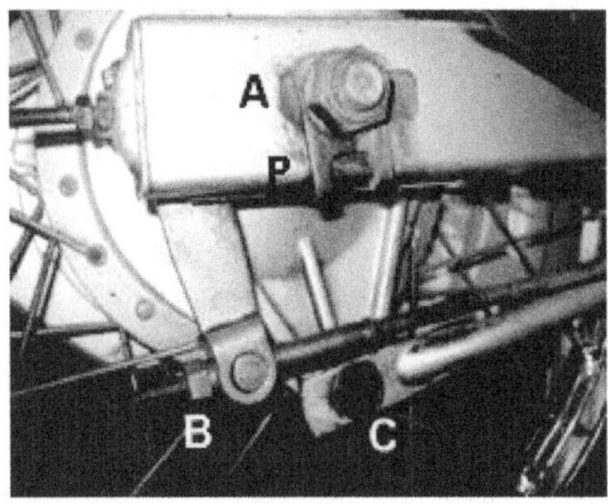

2. ·To remove the stopper arm nut, you might have to remove the cotter pin/split pin.

·Cotter/Split pins need to be replaced every time they are removed. So before you remove them, or if it's missing on your bike, buy a few pins (they cost very little). Make sure you tell the seller where you intend to use the pin, as they come in different sizes.

·Remove the cotter pin by simply pulling it out by holding it at the closed end using pliers and pull it out as pointed out in the picture.

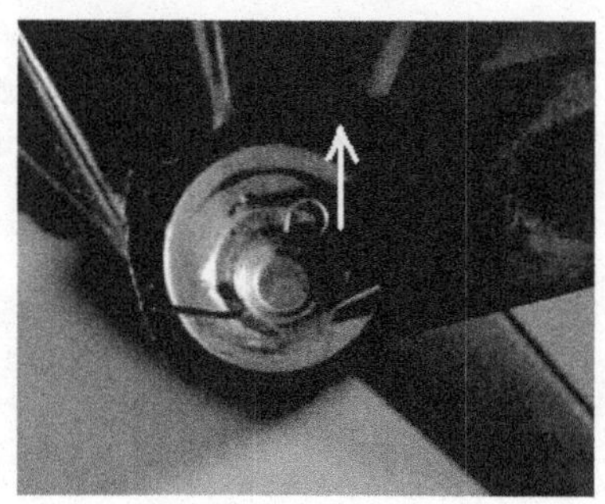

3. ·To remove the brake adjusting nut, push the brake arm forward as shown in the picture and unscrew the nut B.

·Take care not to lose the joint pin.

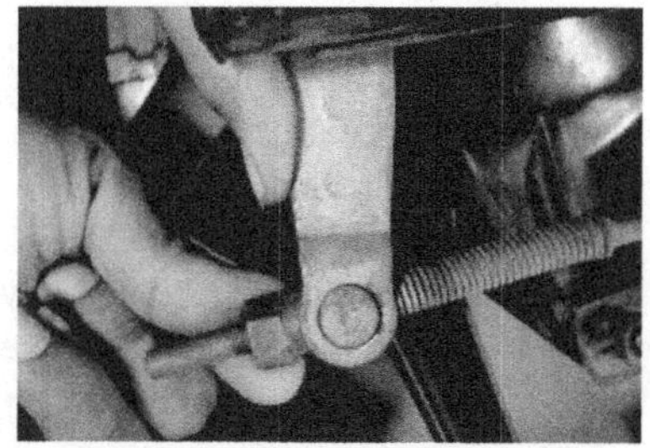

4. ·After following the above steps and removing the nuts, will see the rear axle as shown in the picture.

·Hit the axle with a hammer gently until you see the axle coming out form the other side of the wheel.

5.   ·Once you can see the axle sliding out from the other side, like shown in the figure, pull it out.

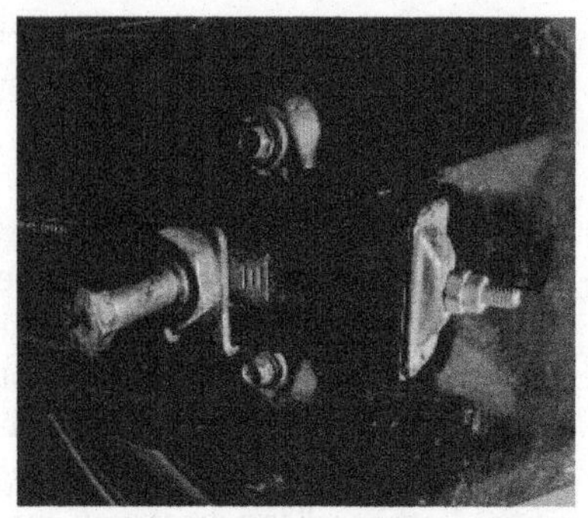

6.   ·Use a hammer if you have to, and gently hit the bolt outwards to help pull the axle out.

·Once you pull the axle out, your rear wheel is free to be taken out.

7.   ·You can simply pull the wheel out by slightly tilting the bike if you have to.

·You will notice that the wheel is attached to the bike via the driven flange shown in the picture.

8.   ·When you pull the axle bolt out, you will note that the side collar shown here and the adjusting plate shown in the first picture will drop off from the bike. Make sure you don't lose them.

9. ·After taking out the wheel you will see that you can remove the drum brake panel out of the hub as shown in the picture by simply lifting it out.

10. ·On the other side of the wheel you will see a setup like the one shown in the picture.

11. ·Before removing the damping rubbers, note the way they are seated in the wheel.

12. ·The black rubber pieces are called the damper rubbers. They soften the shock transmitted from the drive flange to the wheel.

·Pull the rubber dampers out and take a look at their shape.

13. ·If you look at the bike, you will find that the drive flange has four bosses as shown in the picture. These bosses sit in the grooves between the damping rubbers on the wheel.

Your engine drives the chain. The chain turns the rear (driven) sprocket. The drive flange in the previous picture is attached the driven sprocket. So as the sprocket rotates, flange rotates too, which in turn rotates the wheel. The purpose of the damping rubbers is to cushion the transfer of power between the flange and the wheel.

To refit the rear wheel, simply follow the above steps in the reverse order while making sure you take care of the following points.

1. ·Before inserting the brake panel into the hub, make sure the drum surface is clean and has no grease or dirt.

2. ·Make sure that the grooves between the damping rubbers are perfectly alligned to the bosses on the drive flange while fitting the wheel.

3. ·Before inserting the axle bolt, make sure you have placed the adjusting plate and the side collar in place.

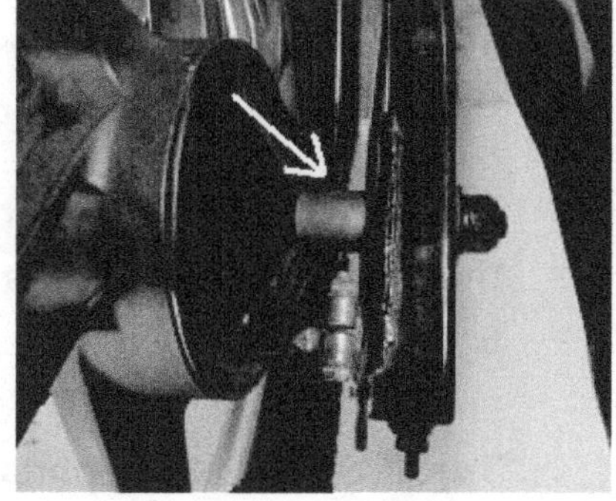

4.   ·Apply grease to the axle bolt before inserting it. Also apply some grease to the inner surface of the sleeve.

·Then tighten the axle nut. **[Torque: 68Nm]**

·Tighten the stopper arm nut. **[Torque: 22Nm]**

·To replace the cotter pin, simply insert the it through the hole on the bolt. After inserting the pin, split the open end.

·After installing the rear wheel, check if the rear brake is working fine. Adjust play if necessary by rotating the adjusting nut.

Maintenance

Wheels are the most important element in your bike but ironically they are also the least bothered about parts. Maintaining wheels is very important to ensure your safety and the bike's performance.

Wheel maintenance is very easy and won't take any time at all. The following is a list of things that you need to take care of:

Tyre Pressure: The importance of checking tyre pressure regularly cannot be overstated. Tire pressure directly affects your bike's fuel efficiency. It affects handling, suspension, tyre life, braking etc.

Under-inflated tyres drink up a lot of fuel, they get heated up quickly, wear prematurely. And over inflated tyres reduce the effectiveness of suspension and transmit shocks to both your bike and your back. Also, over inflated tyres are more prone to punctures and impact damages.

The correct tyre pressure for your bike is:

Front   **25psi**

Rear (Driver only)   **33psi**

Rear (Driver and Pillion)   **41psi**

NOTE: Always check tyre pressure when the tyres are cold. Because tyres get hot as you ride, you need to get it checked before you have driven more than 2-3 kilometres. Also, you are better off not paying attention to any free advice the "tyre pressure guy" might offer. Surely Honda knows better.

It is advisable to check tyre pressure frequently, twice or thrice a month. As a general rule, if the pressure drops by more than 2psi in a month, it means there is something wrong with your tyre. If this keeps happening, it is advisable to get your tyre(s) checked at an authorised service centre.

Also check if your wheels still have their valve caps, if they don't, go buy them and screw them on. They might seem to be insignificant, but they do a good job protecting the valves from dirt, oil and rust causing moisture.

Visual inspection: Visually checking your tyres is a good practice. Simply take a close look at the tyres while rotating them. Look for any embedded objects like nails or stone chips, etc. If you see a fabric like material sticking out or deep cracks or humps, you should have your tyre(s) checked at an authorised service centre.

Also, see how your tyre is wearing. It should wear more at the centre. And it should also be wearing uniformly. If it is not, it could mean improper tyre pressure, faulty suspension, rims, etc in which case you should consult a Honda service centre. It is essential to keep an eye on thread depth as well. Thread depth is

Front tire	**1.5mm**
Rear tire	**2.0mm**

Wheel Bearings: During every periodic service, check the condition of wheel bearings on both the wheels. To check, hold the tire tightly and try to move the wheel side to side (for front wheel you need to make sure the handle doesn't move). If it moves, check where that movement is from. If it is from the bearings, they need to be changed. Also, rotate the wheel and listen for any unusual noises emanating from the bearings. This is also a sign of bearing wear. If your bearings are badly worn, you will also notice the wheel wobbling. While driving you will notice that, when slowing down your bike (braking) or when you ride into a ditch your bike moves like a drunkard. In such case, or if you suspect something wrong with your bearings, you need to get them checked.

Cleaning: However pointless it might seem, it is important to clean your tyres (or rather wash your tyres) once in a while. It is not for aesthetics, but to get rid of any grease, oil, petrol or brake dust from the tyres. These substances damage rubber, so it makes sense to wash them away. Cleaning tyres can be done by simple soapy water and a brush. You can clean the rims too while you are at it.

If you are using a hard brush, just make sure you don't use it to clean your alloy wheels. Use a rag and soapy water to clean rims (both alloy and spoke). After cleaning, pat them dry with a cloth.

Spokes: If your bike has spoked wheels, you need to check them during every servicing schedule. Spokes can get loose or bent over time due to impact and harsh driving conditions. If one spoke gets loose or bent, the others will shortly follow. So, check the spokes occasionally and if you find any loose spokes, get them tightened or buy yourself a spoke wrench. And if you find bent/damaged spokes, get them replaced immediately.

Brakes

We won't bother you by explaining how important brakes are and other such obvious information. But we will take the liberty to stress upon the importance of maintaining them on a regular basis.

Your bike has Hydraulic Disk brake on the front and Drum brake on the rear wheel. Both types of brakes use friction to stop your wheel(s) from rotating. In order to generate enough friction to stop a fast moving bike, brakes use high friction materials on pads or liners. These materials convert the kinetic energy of the bike into heat and then dissipate it back to the atmosphere.

This braking process obviously wears off the friction materials. And this wear can seriously affect your bike's braking. Apart from wear, due to excessive use and the massive heat generated during braking, the pads and brake liners "glaze". It means, they become excessively smooth (glass like), which makes them useless for braking. You will know that glazing has happened if your brake pads/liners don't appear to be worn, but the braking is bad and you might hear a squeaking sound.

So, in order to keep your bike's braking in absolutely reliable condition, regular brake maintenance is very important. The good news is that it's quite easy to maintain your brakes. Simply follow the instructions in this chapter to learn how.

Front brakes

Disk Brakes work a lot like bicycle brakes. If you remember, when you apply brakes on your cycle, two small pads press the cycle tyre from both sides. Disk brakes work just like that. Only, instead of pressing on the tyre, they press against a disk attached to the wheel. And because bikes are heavier and faster than cycles, a lot more force has to be applied to stop the wheel from rotating. To help you apply that extra force, disk brakes are hydraulically assisted.

It is also interesting to know why disk brakes are usually attached to the front wheels and not the rear wheels (even in cars). Why can't we have disk brakes on the back and the regular drum brakes on the front? It's because when you "brake", or even decelerate, no matter which brakes you apply, front or back, your bike's weight (including yours) gets transferred to the front wheel. So, you need more force to stop the front wheel than the rear. You need better and effective brakes on the front. Hence you get Disks in the front. It doesn't mean you don't need Disk brakes in the rear; it depends on how powerful your bike is. sports bikes have 2 disk brakes on each wheel.

Now that you know what disk brakes do and a bit more, let us see how each of the components can be removed and also properly maintained.

Removing/Refitting brake disc

Spanner of size 10/Allen key of size 6

Screw locking agent

You wouldn't need to remove the disk frequently but it's advisable to clean it occasionally of any oil sediments and check for rust, especially the bolts that attach the disk to front wheel once in a while. If you find any rust on the bolts, replace them. If the disk is bent visibly never try to get it fixed, simply replace it. It is also a good idea to get your wheel checked for balance and trueness on such an occasion.

1. To remove the disk, you need to remove the front wheel.

   See the Front Wheel section to see how to do it.

2. Take a close look at the disk. It is attached to the wheel by 5 or 6 bolts (depending on your model) as shown in the picture here.

The old models have regular hexagonal bolt heads and the new ones have Allen heads. You will need an Allen key or a suitable socket to remove these bolts.

To remove the disk, it is very important that you follow this procedure:

First, slightly loosen the bolts in the order shown i.e. loosen 1, then 2, 3, 4, 5 and 6. Then go back to 1 and further loosen it and keep repeating this until you remove all the bolts.

Essentially what you are doing is, removing the bolts in a crisscross fashion. By doing so you will evenly relieve the stress on the disk.

While fitting the disk back on, you need to follow the same order. Tighten 1 a little bit first, then 2, 3, 4, 5 and 6. Initially tighten by hand and then a spanner. But make sure you tighten them little by little in the order shown.
If you don't follow this process, the disk will warp due to the uneven force. Warping means, the disk won't remain perfectly circular and flat. And any deformation in the disk can severely affect braking.

3. ·Once you remove the bolts, you will be able to remove the disk as shown in the picture.

To refit the disk, follow the above steps in a reverse order. Before refitting the disk, however, apply some locking agent (sort of glue) to the disk bolts. Also, it is very important that you tighten the bolts **[Torque: 24Nm]** in the procedure explained above.

Removing/Refitting brake pads

Spanner of size 12
Hammer
Screwdriver

Before removing the brake pads, remember that you should not press the brake lever at all untill you have finished refitting. Because when the wheel is removed, the disk wont be there to stop the pads from coming in to contact if brake is applied. If they do press against each other, it takes a lot of effort to prise them apart to refit the wheel.

1. ·To remove the brake pads, you need to pull out the calliper housing **C** (shown in the picture).

·To do this, remove the two mounting bolts pointed out in the picture.

2. ·Once you have pulled the calliper housing out as shown in the picture, you will see that it is connected to a tube.

·This tube connects the calliper housing to a small oil reservoir near the brake lever on the handle.

·There are two pistons located inside the calliper housing. These pistons press the brake pads against the disk, thus stopping the bike.

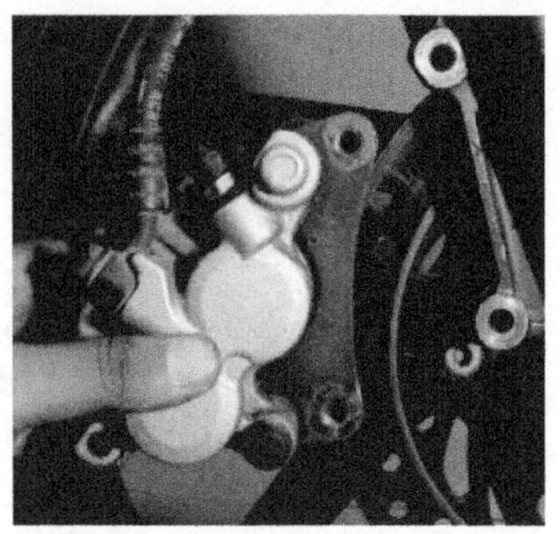

3. ·If you turn the calliper housing around, you will find a clip as shown in the picture (circle).

·This clip locks in place a small metal rod called the Pad Pin to which the brake pads are connected.

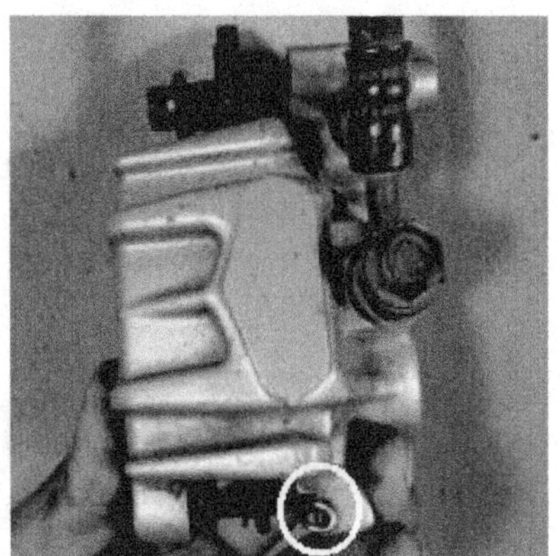

4. ·To remove the pads you need to pull the clip out. Use a screwdriver or pliers if you have to.

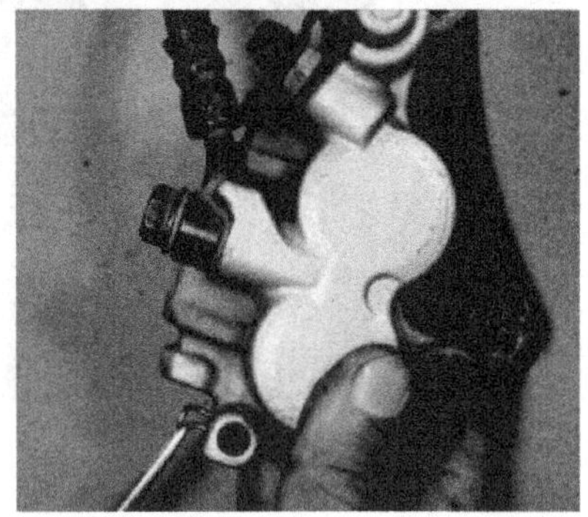

5. ·The Pad Pin needs to be removed next. It is the small metal rod shown by letter P in the picture.

·To remove it, you need to push it out from the direction shown in the picture.

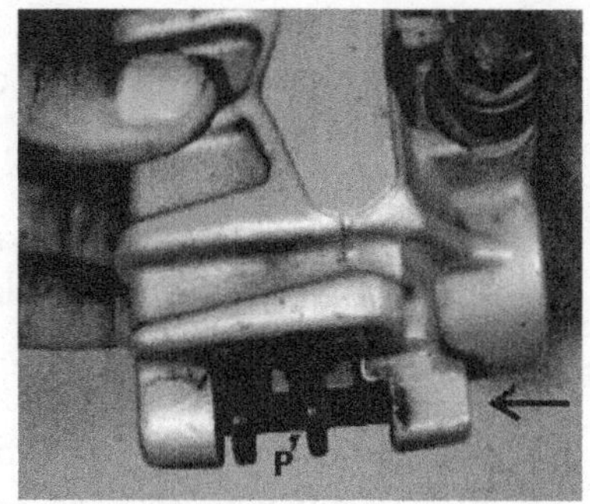

6. · If you look at the calliper in the direction shown above, you will find a small hole as shown in the picture.

·Insert a nail or something similar into this hole and hit it gently with a hammer.

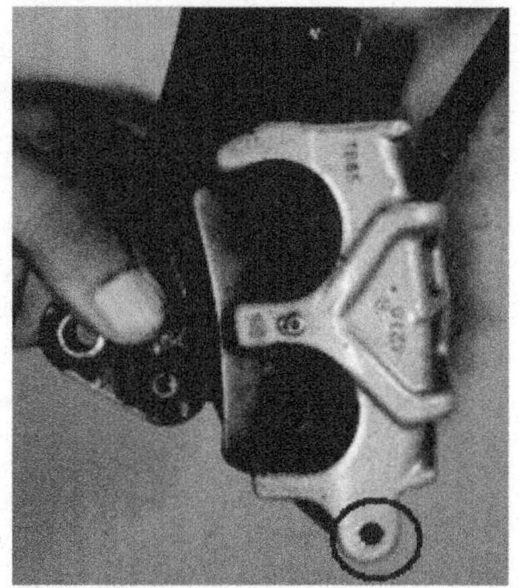

7. ·As soon as you hit, the Pad Pin will start coming out from the other side as shown in the picture.

·Now gently pull it out and the pads will fall right out of the housing.

8. · You will see that a small metal plate as shown in the centre might also fall off.

· This plate is called pad spring and it holds the pads in place.

· Also observe that the two pads are not identical. The one on the right sits near the pistons and the longer one sits on the other end.

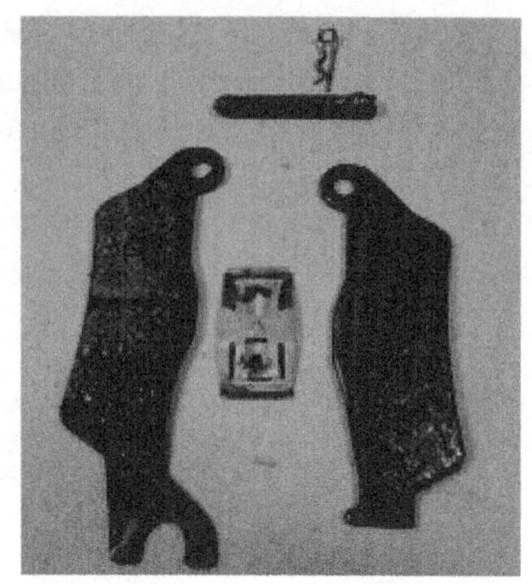

To refit the brake pads follow the above steps in the reverse order while carefully following below points.

9. ·If you are replacing the pads with new ones, you will have to push the pistons (pointed out in the picture) inside a little.

·You should be able to push them by hand if you have strong thumbs. If you can't, proceed and fit the pads first and then stick a screwdriver between them and then prise them apart.

10. ·While refitting, you need to place the pad spring in place.

·Place the spring as shown in the picture.

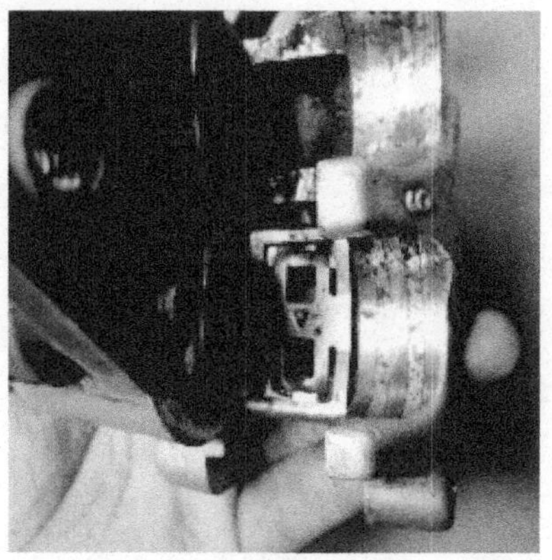

11. ·Now insert the shorter the pad in place (near the pistons).

12. ·Then insert the second pad.

·Make sure that the boss on the calliper housing sits in the groove on the brake pad as shown in the picture.

13. ·Then insert the Pad Pin to lock the pads in position in the same way you have removed it as shown in the picture.

    ·You may have to hit it gently to help it snap into place.

14. ·Insert the clip in its position to prevent the pad pin from slipping out

    ·Now you can refit the calliper housing by tightening the two mounting bolts **[Torque: 30Nm]**.

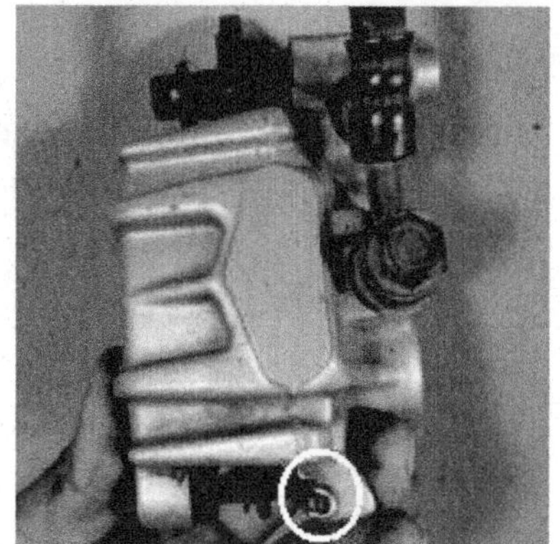

Maintenance

Disk brakes are designed to be maintenance free, but there a few tasks that need to be carried out to ensure proper working and your safety. These tasks are, checking the brake fluid level and checking brake pad wear. Replacing brake fluid is only required every 2 years and requires a certain amount of skill and preferably proper equipment. So we have chosen not to include that topic here as it is beyond the scope of this book.

Brake fluid level check

Brake fluid enhances and transmits the force applied by you at the lever to the pistons in the calliper housing. The entire system is made air-tight to ensure its efficiency. So, your brake fluid doesn't get used up. The amount of brake fluid will remain constant. But, as the brake pads wear, the pistons will move forward and rest at a further position and hence the level of brake fluid falls. So, after replacing them with new pads, the fluid level will come back to normal.

If there is a leak however, you need to get the problem fixed. After fixing the leak problem, you need to completely bleed the old brake fluid out and replace it with fresh fluid. This is because brake fluid absorbs moisture when it comes into contact with air and becomes unusable.

1. ·Checking your brake fluid level is straightforward. Simply check if the fluid level falls below the MIN marking on the reservoir.

    · Check the level when the reservoir is parallel to the ground. To do this, turn the handle until the reservoir is roughly parallel to the ground.

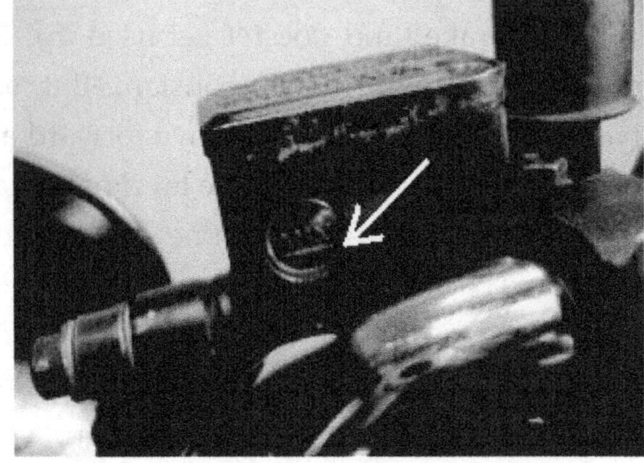

·If the level is on or below the MIN marking, it means either your pads are worn or that there is a leak in the system.

·To check pad wear, read the following section. If the pads are fine then there is most likely a leak in the system, in which case you need to contact an authorised Honda service centre.

Brake pads wear inspection

Brake pads work their magic through friction. Imagine the amount of abrasion and heat that is created while stopping a disk rotating at high speed. All this hard work will wear the pads over time. So, brake pads' wear needs to be checked during every servicing schedule.

Check brake pad wear by following instructions here and if they are worn out, replace them by following the instructions in the section on Brake Pad Replacement.

- To ckeck brake pad wear, bend down and look at the pads. You will be able to see notches on the pads as pointed out in the picture. Clean the brake calliper and the pads if they are too dirty.

- If you can see the notches, it means the pads are fine. If the pads have worn so much that these nothes have gone, it means you need to replace the pads.

- If you can't find the notches but are not sure, you should probably pull the calliper out of the disk. Refer the brake pad removal section to learn how it's done.

- Once you remove the brake calliper from the bike, look at the pads closely to find the notches as shown in the picture.

- If you can't see them, it's time to replace the pads.

Rear brakes

Removing/Refitting

You need to remove the rear wheel first in order to remove the rear brake panel assembly. Please go back to the Rear wheel section and have a look at how the wheel is removed.

 Note that, the dust in the brake hub and on the panel has asbestos in it which can be very dangerous if inhaled. Don't blow air on to the brake pads or the hub. Use a rag made wet with diesel to do the cleaning.

Please don't forget to wear gloves.

1. ·When you apply rear brake by pressing the brake pedal, it pulls the brake rod to the right.

    ·And the brake rod pulls the brake arm attached to it.

    ·Try pressing the brake pedal and see what these parts do. You will note that the brake rod makes the brake arm move forward and backward as shown by the arrows.

    ·And when the lever moves forward, brake is applied. To understand how this actually works, let's have a look inside.

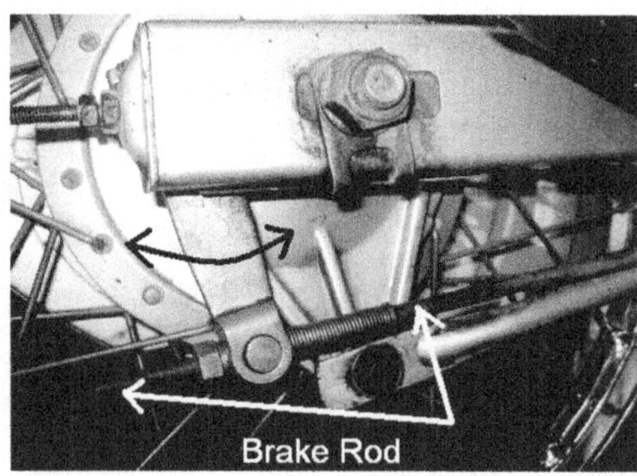

2. ·See Rear Wheel chapter to know how to get the rear wheel out.

·Remove the brake shoe assembly from the wheel as shown in the picture.

·Note that, the hole in which the brake shoes sit is called the brake drum.

3. ·Take the brake shoe assembly out and have a look at it. Before we remove the brake shoes, let's see how these drum brakes work.

·In the beginning of the section we have seen that, when you press the brake pedal, the brake arm moves back and forth as shown in the picture.

·Now that we have the whole mechanism taken out, try moving the brake arm back and forth as shown by the arrows.
·You will see that as you move the arm, the two brake shoes move outwards as shown by the arrows.

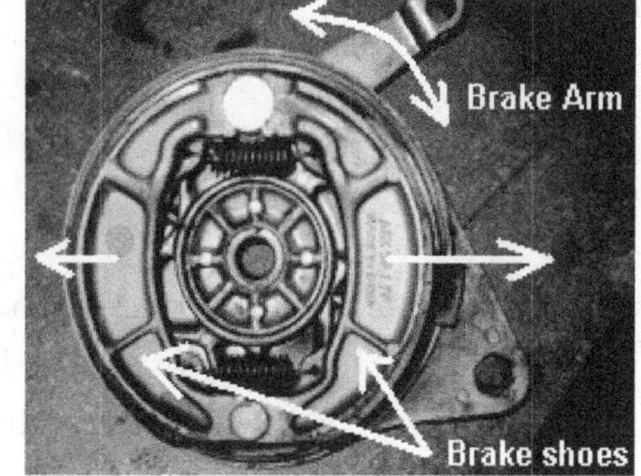

·As the shoes move out in the direction shown, they press against the brake drum. And because of friction between them, the wheel stops.

4.
·To remove the brake shoes, you simply need to push one out with your thumb as shown in the picture.

·Also note that the outer surface of the shoes rubs against the brake hub when brakes are applied.

·And due to the friction, the wheel slowly stops rotating.

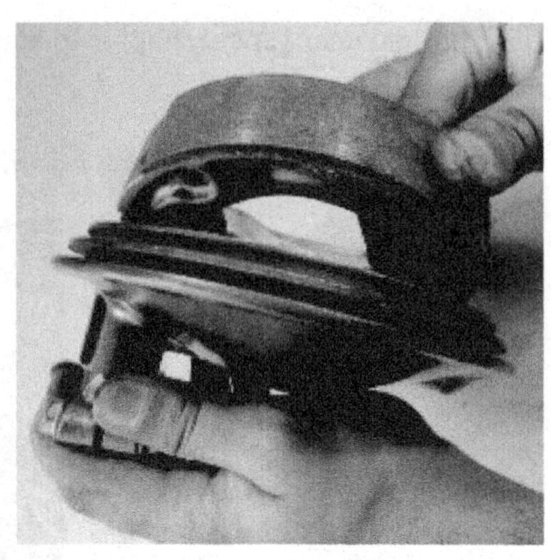

5.
·Once you have separated the shoes like in the picture here, observe their shape, particularly their ends.

·They both have a flat face on one end and they have a circular groove on the other end as pointed out in the picture.

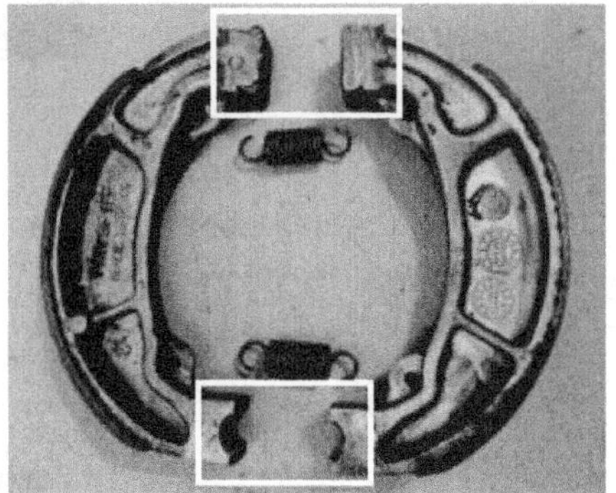

Re-assembling the brakes is an easy task, but you might feel it's a bit tricky if you are doing it for the first time. Make sure you follow the below points carefully.

1. ·Now to re-assemble the brakes, hook the springs on to the shoes as shown in the picture.

   ·Once you have hooked up the springs, the shoes should look like in the picture.

   ·Make sure that the ends of both shoes match, i.e. the flat faces (1) and the semi-circular grooves (2) as shown in the picture.

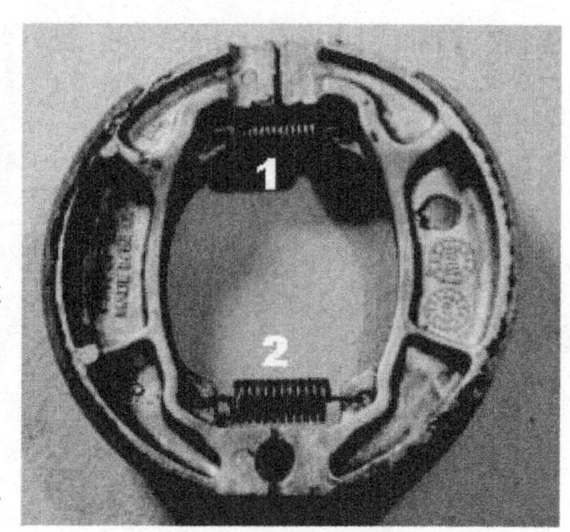

2. ·Before refitting the shoes, it is a good idea to apply some multi-purpose grease to the brake cam (**1**) and the anchor pin (**2**).

   ·While getting the shoes back on, make sure you match the ends properly. The flat faces on the shoes should align with the brake cam's sliding surface.

   ·And the grooved ends in the picture above should sit around the anchor pin.

3. ·In order to put the shoes back on, hold the shoes one in each hand.

·Now move the shoes with your hands as if you were closing a book.

Now push both ends on as shown in the picture.

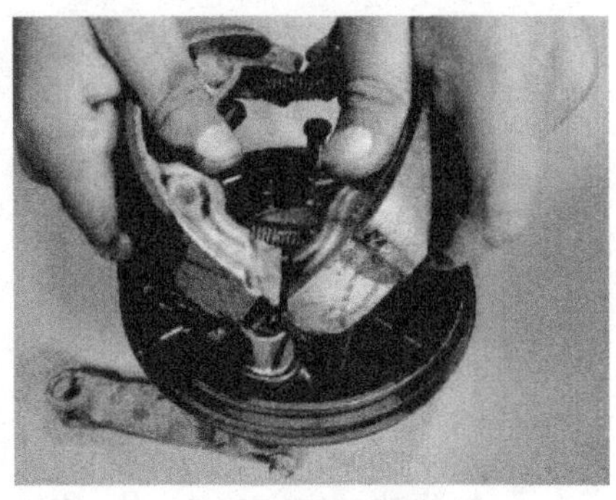

4. ·Once they are on, push them down to their original position as shown in the picture.

Maintenance

Rear brake Play adjustment

1. ·Rear brake play is the distance travelled by the brake pedal before the brake is actually applied.

   ·Ideally this play should be 2-3centimetres. However, bikers often have different personal opinions when it comes to play.

   ·But make sure the play is never so little that you end up brake riding all the time.

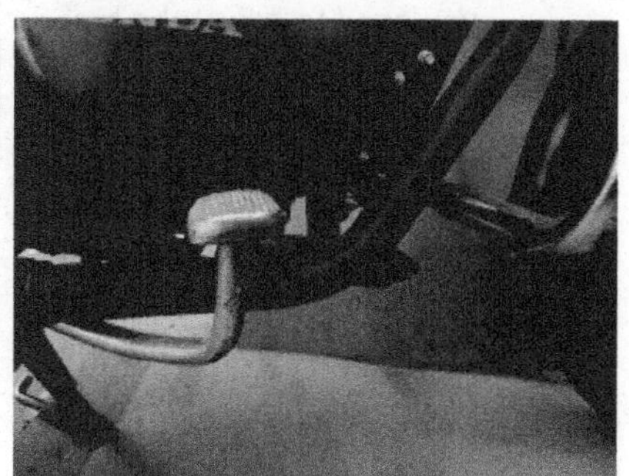

2. ·To adjust the play, rotate the adjusting screw shown in the picture.

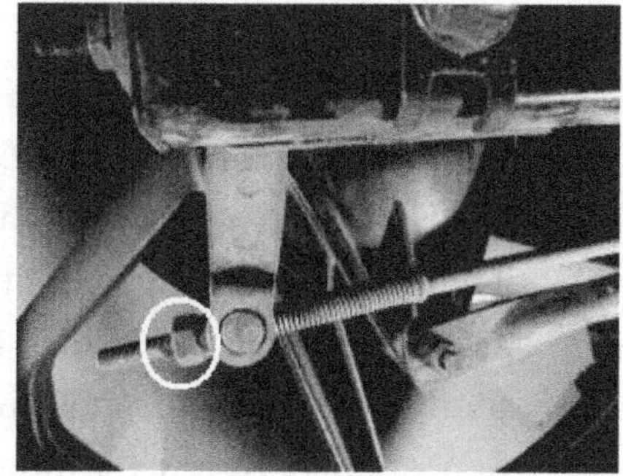

3. ·After you have adjusted the brake play, check if the brake light turns on precisely when the brake pedal is pressed.

·If the brake light is constantly glowing or if it turns on late, you need to adjust the brake light adjuster.

·It is located behind the aluminium panel that supports the right side rear footrest.

·To adjust, simply rotate the nut shown in the picture while holding the switch body.

·Check if the brake light is working properly again.

Rear brake liners' wear

Brakes work due to the friction between the brake liners and the brake drum. Because of repeated rubbing between the two surfaces, the brake liners get worn out. The amount of wear obviously depends on how often and how hard the brakes are applied. Also, because the brake drums are not air tight, dirt and grime gets deposited between the liner and the drum. This also wears off the lines and drum.

So, to maintain your brakes in proper and safe condition you need to check their wear regularly and clean them. Brake maintenance is easy and doesn't take much time.

1. ·Check your rear brakes for wear occasionally. There is a provision on your bike that tells you when your brake liners are worn out.

·Take a look at the rear wheel to find the setup shown in the picture.

·Press the brake pedal and see if the pointer on the right reaches the reference mark on the left. If it does, it means it's time to replace your brake shoes.

·Older models have slightly different but easily understandable setup.

2. ·Refer rear brake removal section and remove the brake shoes.

3. ·The top surface of the shoes pointed out in the picture is called the brake liner.

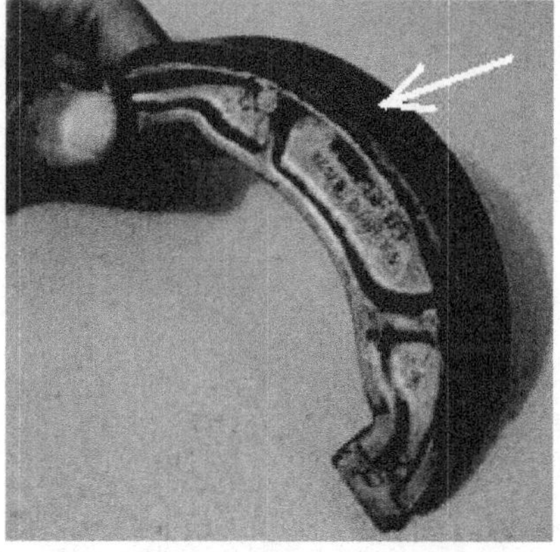

4. ·To clean the liners, use a sandpaper and rub away any dirt or grime that is accumulated on the liners as shown in the picture

5. ·Then using the sand paper, wipe the inside of brake drum as shown in the picture.

6. ·Also clean the other parts of the brake using sand paper and a cloth moistened with diesel.

Chain and Sprockets

The chain on your bike is an important element which transfers the power from your engine to the drive wheel (the rear wheel). For a moment imagine the amount of force required to push your bike forward with you sitting on it. Now imagine the force required to push it at 40kmph, or to push it up a slope with a heavy friend sitting behind you. That is how much load your bike's chain has to take every time you drive. So the next time your chain snaps, don't swear at the poor thing; show some concern. You might be surprised to know that the chain loses only 1% of its efficiency due to friction despite having a large number of mating parts.

Removing/Refitting

Chain enclosure

T Spanner of size 10

1. ·Have a look at the chain enclosure as shown in the picture.

   ·Note the position of the 4 small screws marked by the circles.

2. ·The chain enclosure is made up of two halves. The top and bottom covers.

   ·Once you remove all the four screws you should be able to pull out the covers.

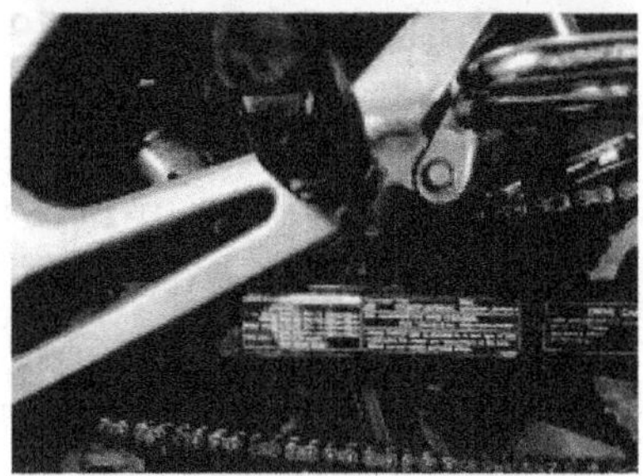

Refitting the chain enclosure is the reverse of the process explained so far.

Sometimes the enclosure covers get bent and starts rubbing against the chain. This produces a peculiar grinding sound whenever the bike moves. So to fix this problem, have a look at the covers and see if there is a dent or bend. You can straighten it by hand or by flattening it on ground by hitting it with a hammer or preferably a piece of wood.

Chain

Pliers (preferably long nose pliers)

T Spanner of size 8

A screwdriver

1 ·To remove the chain, you need to remove the chain enclosure by following the instructions in the previous section.

·Then, remove the two bolts shown in the picture to remove the crank case cover.

·Removing this cover will gain you access to the drive (front) sprocket.

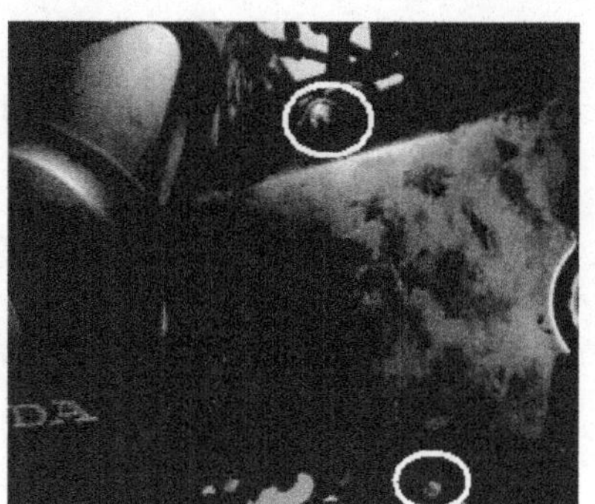

2. ·To remove the chain, first wipe the chain with a cloth as you rotate the wheel so that you can see all the links clearly.

·Now by slowly rotating the wheel, find a link which looks different from the others.

·You will see that it has a circular slot and looks like the one shown in the picture.

·It is called the chain's Master Link. To remove the chain you need to remove the Master link.

·Rotate the wheel until this link comes to the top of rear sprocket. Then get your bike into the 1st gear. By doing this your chain will remain where it is.

3. · The master link is made up of 3 pieces:

The Master Link M

The link plate P

Link Lock L

And C is the actual chain.

They are attached to the chain in the orientation shown in the picture here.

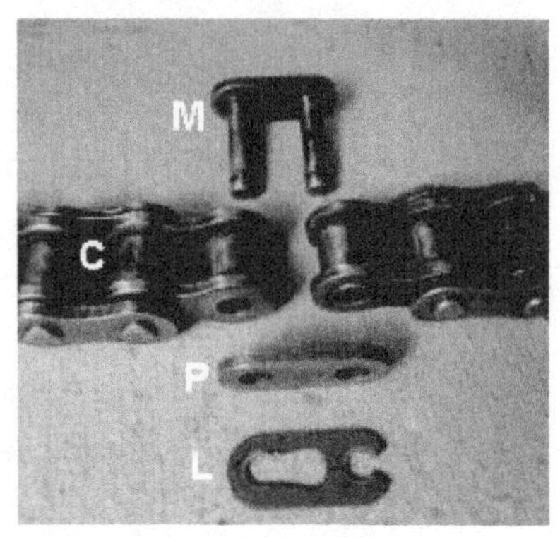

4. ·Here is a closer view of the link lock.

·As you can see, the lock is a simple, C shaped piece of metal.

·If you expand it in the direction shown, it will slip off the master link.

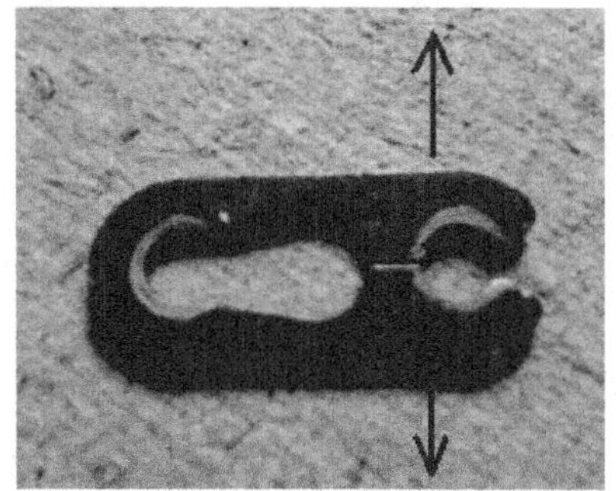

5. ·Stick a screwdriver on the open end side and push it as shown in the picture. This will push the link lock out.

·Make sure you don't lose it, because sometimes it flies off as soon as you release it.

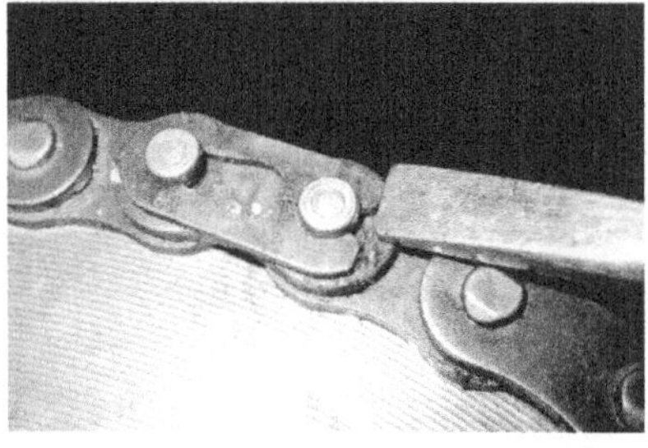

6. ·After removing the link lock you can remove the retaining plate and the master link by simply pulling them out.

·When you pull out the master link, the chain will simply be free to remove.

·Get your bike in to neutral and just pull out the chain.

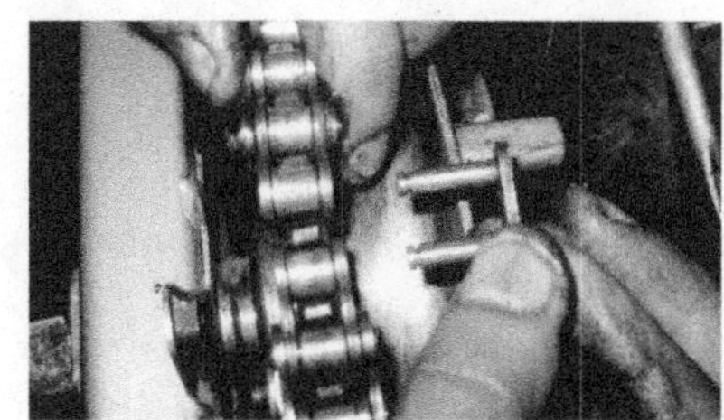

7. ·While refitting the chain, make sure the chain sits around the front sprocket first and then, wind it around the rear sprocket. When you bring the two open ends together as shown here, get your bike into 1st gear again.

8. ·Now follow the removal steps in reverse order.

·It is a little tricky to get the link lock to sit in position.

·To do this, get a set of pliers or nose pliers if you have them and then press the link lock into its position by holding it as shown in the picture.

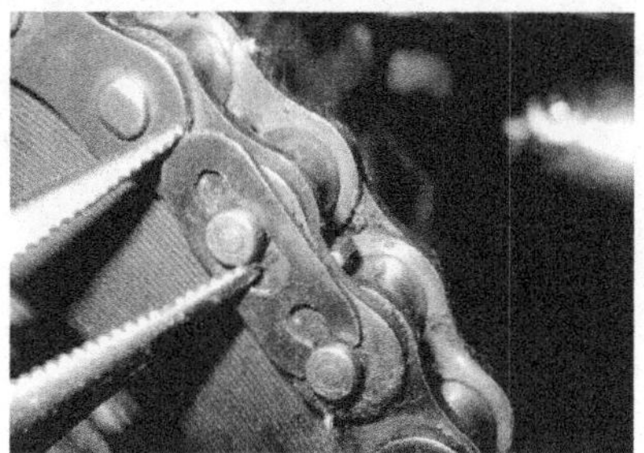

Drive sprocket

 T Spanner of size 10

If the drive sprocket is worn, it is advisable to replace sprockets and chain as a set. Using an old chain on new sprockets or vice versa will wear all of them rapidly. The following steps will show you how to remove the drive sprocket.

1. ·First put the bike in first gear.

   ·Then remove the gear shift pedal/lever by removing the pinch bolt as shown in the picture.

   ·After removing the bolt you can simply pull the gear lever out.

2. ·Remove the two bolts shown in the picture to remove the crank case cover.

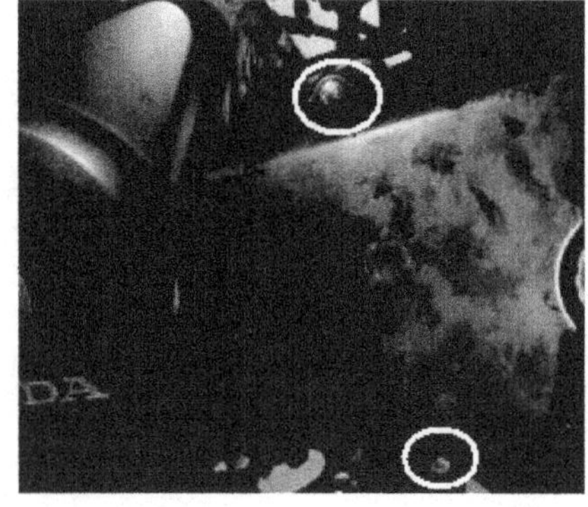

3. ·After removing the cover, you will see that the sprocket is held in place by a fixing plate and 2 bolts.

·Remove these two bolts.

4. ·After removing the two bolts, turn the fixing plate as shown in the picture and then pull it out.

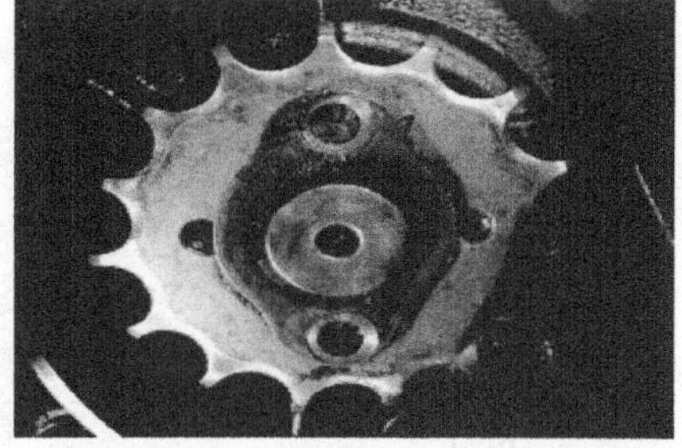

5 ·After removing the fixing plate, you can remove the sprocket by pulling it out.

To refit the sprocket, follow the steps above in the reverse order. Make sure that the sprocket's face with markings on it should face you, place the fixing plate and tighten the drive sprocket bolts **[Torque: 12Nm].**

Driven sprocket

 Spanners of sizes 31 and 14

If your sprocket needs to be replaced due to wear, it is advisable to replace it as a set along with a new chain and drive (front) sprocket. Using an old chain on new sprockets or vice versa will wear all of them rapidly.

1. ·To remove the rear sprocket, you need to remove the rear wheel, the chain covers and the chain. Please see the respective sections to learn how to do these.

   ·Once these are done, you need to remove the sleeve nut shown in the picture.

2. ·After removing the sleeve nut, the sprocket should look like this.

3. ·To remove the rear sprocket, you simply need to pull out the sprocket from behind (as shown in the picture)

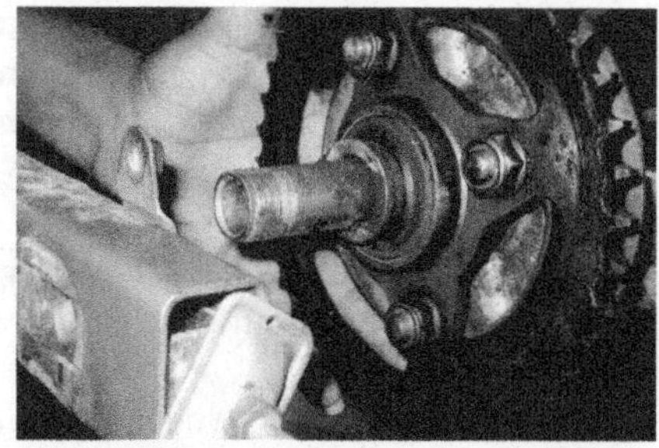

4. ·Then remove the collar as shown in the picture.

5. ·Now, pull the axle sleeve from behind as shown in the picture.

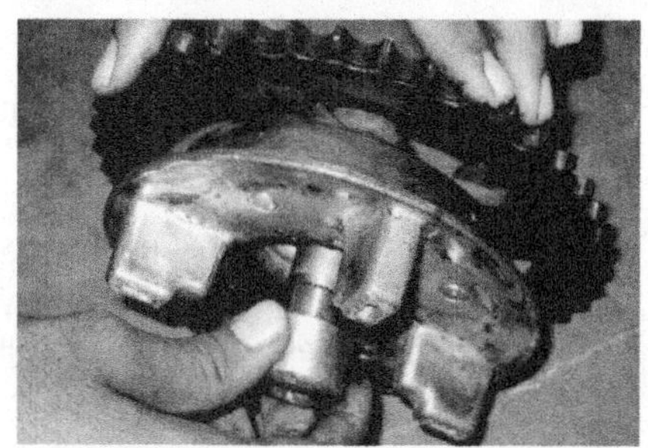

6. ·You will note that the sprocket is actually bolted on to the driven flange.

·To separate the sprocket you need to remove the four nuts shown here.

7 ·These nuts are rather tight and it's quite tricky to get a grip on the sprocket in order to remove the nuts.

·To make this easy however, there is a small trick.

·Place the rear wheel flat on the ground (brake drum facing down) after removing the rear brake panel (refer to the Rear Wheel chapter).

·Now, place the sprocket and driven flange assembly on the wheel by aligning the bosses on the flange with the grooves between the rubber dampers.

8. ·Then, sit with your knees pressing on the tyre as shown in the picture.

·This will solidly hold the sprocket and you can apply enough leverage to remove all the screws.

·While removing the bolts, do so in steps. Gradually loosen opposite bolts and repeat until all 4 bolts come free.

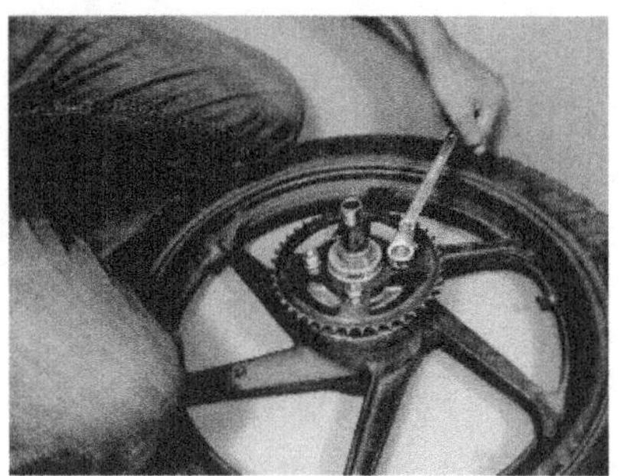

To refit the sprocket, you need to follow the removal instructions in reverse order. Before proceeding, take note of the following points.

9. ·While refitting the sprocket on to the driven flange, the face with lettering on it should face you and the other face will mate with the driven flange.

·Tighten the driven sprocket nuts [Torque: 64Nm]

·Then insert the axle sleeve and the collar as shown in the picture.

Maintenance

The chain is the driving element of your bike. It takes quite a battering, so frequent maintenance is advisable. Maintenance mainly involves, cleaning and lubricating regularly.

Lubricating the chain needs to be done frequently, around every 500km. You can find the oil at any auto spares shop. Alternatively, you could buy a can of "Chain lube". To lubricate the chain, remove the chain casing as shown in chain the Case Removal section. Then pour oil on to the chain as it goes over the rear sprocket while rotating the rear wheel. Place a rag or paper on the floor to prevent an oil puddle. If you are going to use a chain lube, make sure you hold a piece of cloth or paper to block the spayed lubricant from reaching your alloys (Chain lube can damage the finish).

If you find that the chain has accumulated a lot of dirt and grime, you should clean it. Remove the chain following the instructions in the Chain Removal section. Put it in a bowl (along with the master link) and soak it in diesel for a few minutes. Then brush off all the dirt with a nylon brush or a toothbrush with strong bristles. Dispose the dirty diesel and repeat the process with fresh diesel until you are satisfied.

If this is too messy for your taste, you should try WD40. Spray the chain liberally with WD40 and let it soak for a moment (only a moment, don't let it dry off). Then spray again. You will be surprised how efficiently it drives out all the dirt and grime.

After cleaning, use a cloth to wipe the chain and check if it has any kinked links or for any other damage. If there are a few damaged links, it's advisable to get you bike to a Honda service centre. If it's repairable, they should be able to replace the few links. If they think your chain needs replacement, now you know how to do it anyway. As explained in the previous sections, a worn or damaged chain will cause wear on sprockets also, so beware.

If the chain looks good and shiny, take a minute to appreciate its beauty and design before you put it back on the bike and lubricate it as explained earlier.

Adjusting Chain slack

 Spanners of sizes 31, 22, 10 and 12

Slack is nothing but "looseness" of the chain. It tells you by how much the chain moves up and down between the front and the rear sprockets. Checking chain slack is very important not just to prolong its life, but also for your bike's safety. Ideally the slack should be around 2-3cm (1 inch). If it is more/less than that, you will have to adjust it.

Before we go ahead and see how slackness is adjusted, let us get something clarified. Your chain is fixed at two places, at the drive (front) sprocket and the rear (driven) sprocket. And the chain cannot elongate or contract because its length is fixed. So, to adjust the slackness, we need to move one of the two sprockets. The front sprocket is connected to the gearbox and cannot move. So we are left with the rear sprocket. If the rear sprocket moves towards the front sprocket (front of the bike), chain becomes loose (i.e. slackness increases) and vice versa.

The chain needs to have some slack. It should not be too tight because, when your bike goes over a bump, the swing arm (and hence the rear wheel) moves up and down and hence creates even more tension. This severely damages sprockets and the chain itself. Also, if there is little or no slack, the extra tension wears out sprockets and the chain and can even lead to wheel misalignment.

On the other hand, if there is too much slack, the chain could slip off the sprocket. If this happens, you are in trouble. Often, when a chain slips, it gets wound around the front sprocket and gets struck between the sprocket teeth and the crank case body. And because the sprocket will continue to rotate, it will start grinding the chain mercilessly until eventually damaging the crank case body.

1. ·To check the chain slackness, open the inspection cap as shown in the picture.

   ·Using your finger, lift the chain and check the slack. It should be 2-3cm. If it is more or less, you will have to adjust the slack.

2. ·To adjust the slack, loosen the rear wheel's axle bolt as shown in the picture. Not too much, a couple of turns will do.

3. ·Then, loosen the sleeve nut as shown in the picture.

4. ·Now, take a look at the markings highlighted by the box.
·There are similar markings on the other side also. As you tighten/ loosen the chain, these markings move.

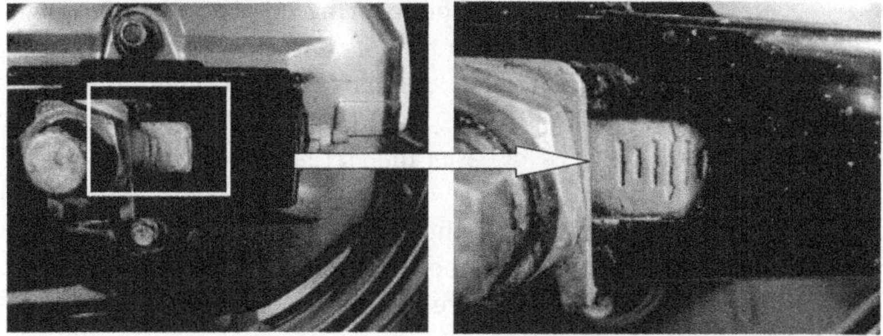

5. ·Finally, to remove the clutch cable completely, you need to pull the button at its end from the lever.

·Simply push the cable down through the slot to slip the button as shown in the picture.

·Now that you have removed one end of the clutch cable let us see how the other end can be released.

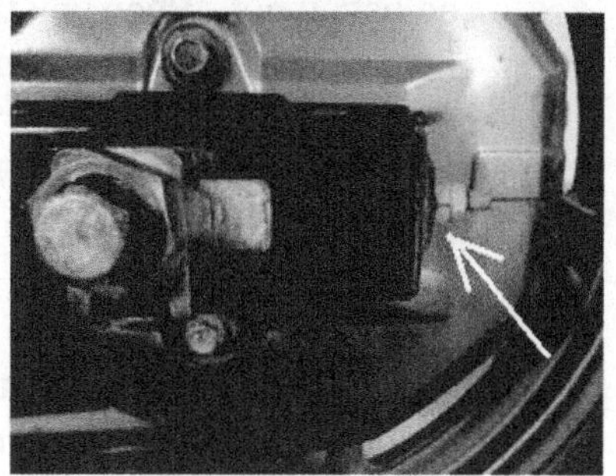

6. ·Here is a close-up of the two nuts. The nut on the left is the adjusting nut and the one on the right is the lock nut.

·As you tighten the adjusting nut, the chain gets tight and vice versa.

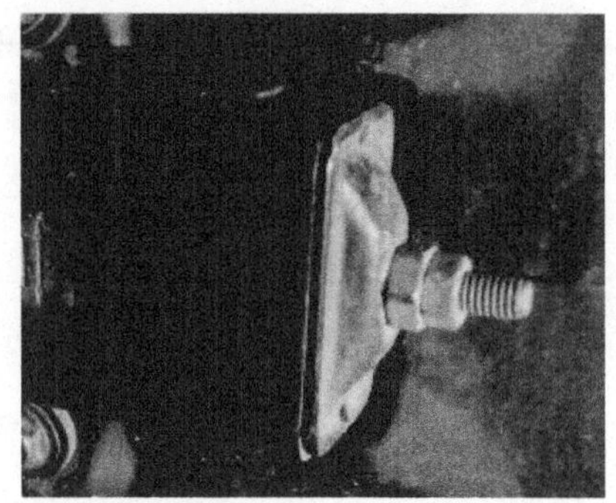

·The lock nut makes sure the adjusting nut stays in place. So, to tighten or loosen the adjusting nut, you need to loosen the lock nut first.

·However, when loosening the chain (by loosening the adjusting nut), you will have to push the rear wheel forward and check the slack. This is because loosening the adjusting nut won't move the rear wheels axle. Don't worry if all this has utterly confused you. It's a lot easier than it reads, we promise.

·And yes, when you push the rear wheel forward, just push it till it stops. If you push it too hard, your bike will think you are trying to get it off the centre stand and will oblige.

·Check the chain slackness as you tighten/loosen the adjusting nut. When you think that the slackness is right, note the reading as shown.

·Now go over to the other side of the wheel. You will find a similar adjusting nut. Turn this nut also to match the readings.

·Check the slack one last time and tighten the lock nuts on both sides while holding the adjusting nut with your other hand. Finally tighten the sleeve nut [Torque: 59Nm] and then the axle nut [Torque: 68Nm].

Sometimes, the readings shown in the pictures may not be visible due to the bike's age or poor maintenance. In such a case, to tighten the chain, tighten the adjusting nut shown in Step 5 making note of how many turns you have turned it. Then check the slackness by lifting the chain with a finger. Say, if the chain slackness is perfect after turning the nut 3 turns, you have to turn the nut on the other side of the wheel 3 times also. It is very important you turn both the nuts the same number of turns. Otherwise, the rear wheel will not be aligned to the front wheel and will lead to loss of balance.

Once you have turned both nuts to adjust the chain slackness, spin the rear wheel and look at it from behind the bike. Make sure it's not wobbling or tilted to one side. If the wheel is fine, turn the wheel again and apply the rear brake suddenly. This will set the wheel in its right position. Now, tighten the sleeve nut and then the axle nut.

Cables

There are four control cables on your bike viz. Clutch cable, Accelerator cable, Speedometer cable and the Choke cable. The basic purpose of these cables is to pass on mechanical force from one place to the other. Like in case of a clutch cable, the pulling force you apply on the clutch lever is transmitted down to the crank case. The same happens in all the cables, force or more importantly the motion is transmitted from one point to other.

Cables are simple steel ropes placed inside a flexible plastic housing/cover. These covers protect the actual rope from damage due to contact and corrosion. These types of cables are called Bowden cables.

Your speedometer cable and choke cable won't give you any problems usually, clutch cable and throttle cables need most of your attention. This is obviously because of their excessive use and the way they work.

Removing/Refitting

Clutch cable

 Spanners of sizes 12 and 14

Clutch cables don't need to be replaced unless they are broken or there is visibly wear i.e. a few strands of wire are cut.

Take a look at the clutch cable connection at the crank case end i.e. near the kick rod. You will see a set-up like the one shown in the picture.

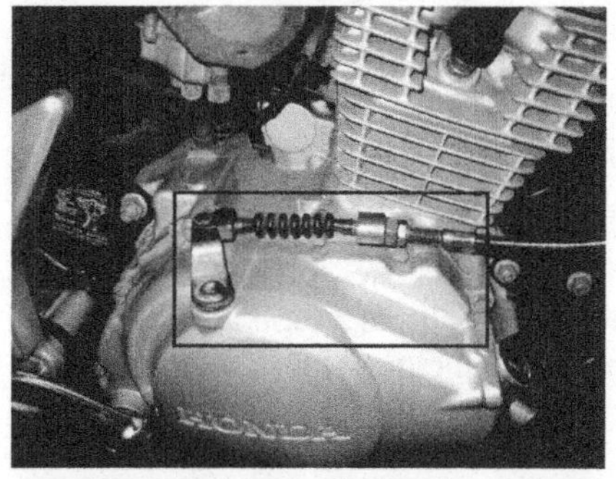

Note the different parts and their names shown in the picture. The adjusting nut is used to adjust the Clutch cable play and the Lock nut is used to prevent the adjusting nut from moving. Also take a

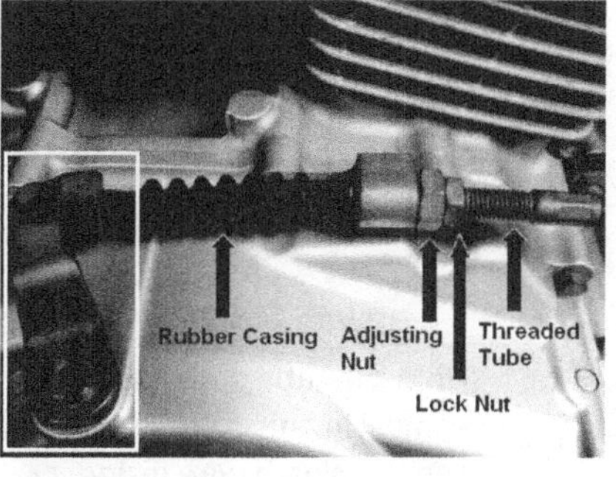

look at the Γ shaped piece of metal highlighted by a box to the left of the picture. This is called Lifter Arm.

While pressing and releasing the clutch lever, observe the movement of Lifter Arm. It moves to the right as the clutch lever is pressed and goes back when you release the lever because of the spiral spring attached to it. So when you press the clutch lever, this lifter arm moves and disengages the clutch.

1. ·To remove/replace clutch cable, loosen the adjuster and lock nuts as shown in the picture.

   ·Now move on to the other end of the clutch cable i.e. near the clutch lever.

2. ·At the Clutch lever, when you pull back the rubber cover, you will see a tube as shown in the picture.

   ·The clutch wire lies inside this tube.

3. ·Hold the tube and pull it out as shown in the picture. You will see the clutch wire inside it.

   ·Also note that, the clutch lever has a slot as shown in the picture.

4. ·The wire needs to be pulled out through this slot.

·Simply slide the wire out while holding the tube as shown in the picture.

5. ·Finally, to remove the clutch cable completely, you need to pull the button at its end from the lever.

·Simply push the cable down through the slot to slip the button as shown in the picture.

·Now that you have removed one end of the clutch cable let us see how the other end can be released.

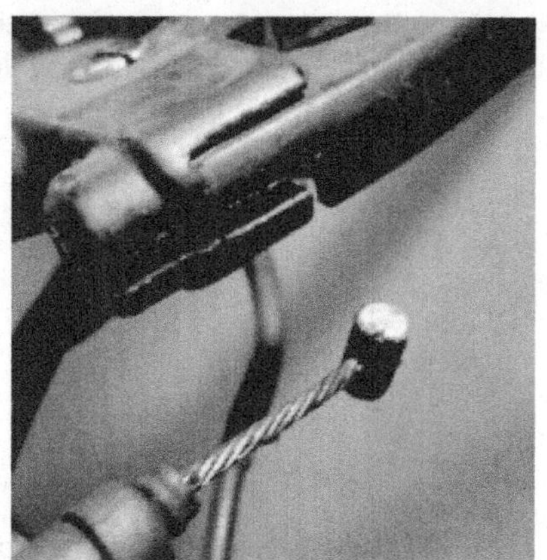

6. ·As you have loosened the adjuster and lock nuts in the beginning, now you need to release the wire from the Lifter arm's slot as shown in the figure. Note that you need to pull the rubber casing (dust cover) back and push the wire toward the lifter arm as shown in the picture.

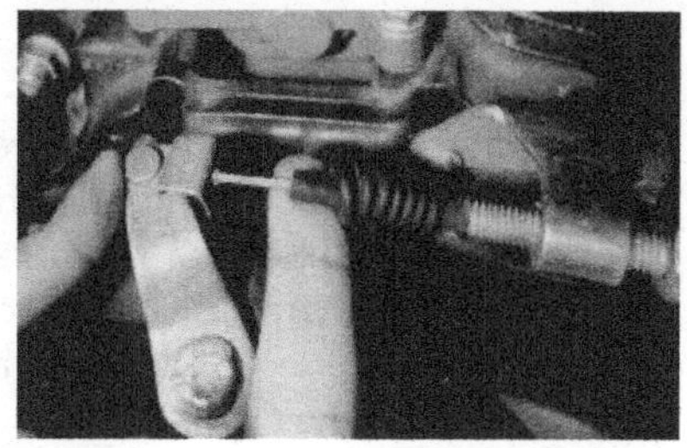

·And while holding the wire with your right hand, push the lifter arm to the right as shown in the picture.

7. ·Then, simply slide the wire upwards to release it from lifter arm as shown in the picture.

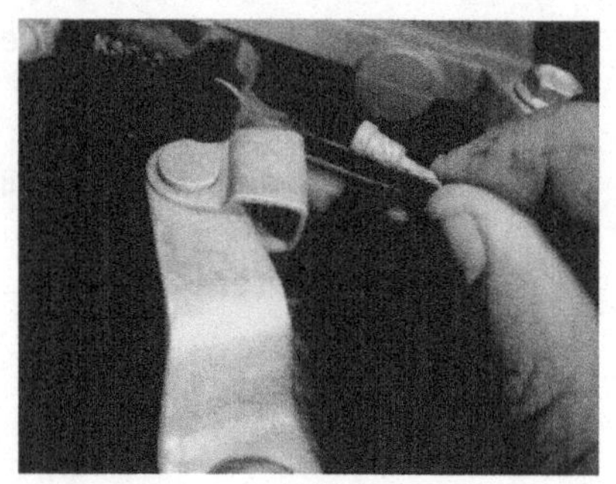

8. ·After releasing the wire form the link you can see that the wire has a small button which sits in the lifter arm slot.

9. ·After releasing the wire from the lifter arm slot, pull the rubber dust cover to your left until you can see the wire inside.

·Then, holding the dust cover back with one hand and the threaded tube with the other hand gently release the clutch wire from under the hook as shown in the picture.

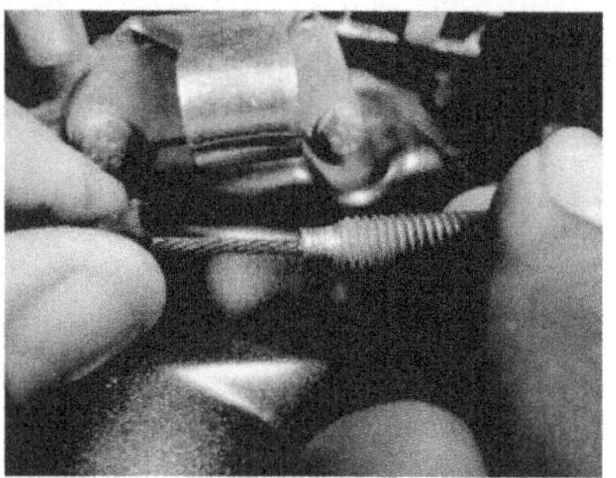

Now as you have successfully released the clutch cable at its both ends, you can simply pull it out. Replacing it with a new one would be straightforward as you know how to connect it at the both ends. Make sure that you route the cable in the same way you have taken it out. It should not obstruct the handle movement at all.

Throttle/Accelerator cable

Spanners of sizes 8,10 and 14

Phillips screwdriver

The accelerator cable looks and works almost exactly like the clutch cable. The only difference is that the rotation of the throttle grip pulls the wire by winding it around and thus pulling the throttle valve open.

1. ·To remove/replace the accelerator cable, you need to open the hub next to the accelerator.

·Hub is the black box next to the accelerator that has the headlight ON/OFF switch on it shown by the arrow.

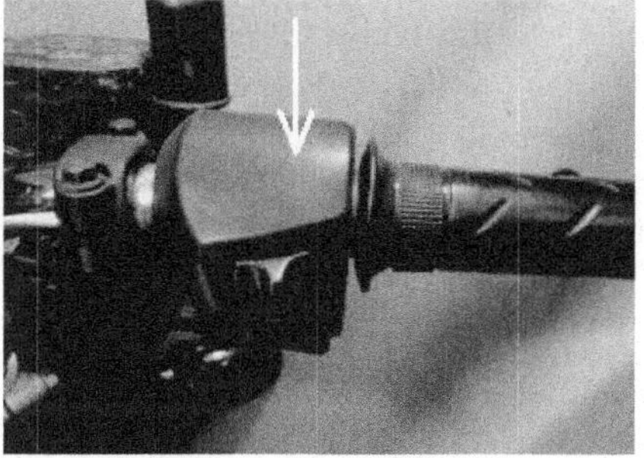

2. ·Look at this hub from below and you will find the two screws shown in the picture here.

   ·Remove these two screws using a Phillips (star) screwdriver.

   ·Also loosen the nut pointed by the arrow in the picture. This nut fixes the accelerator cable to the hub.

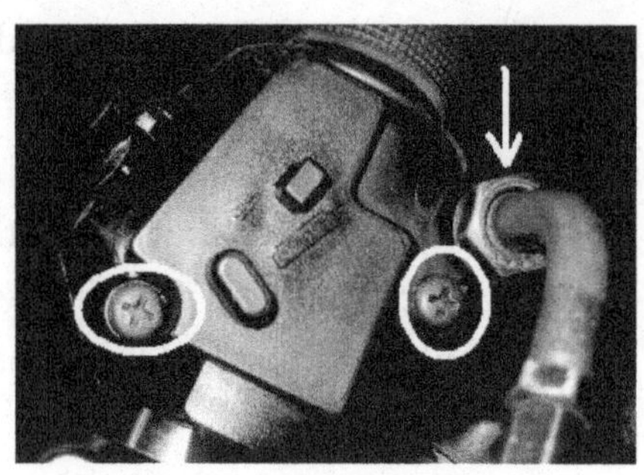

3. ·After you remove the two screws, the hub will split into two halves as shown in the picture.

   ·The top half has electrical wiring connected to it.

   ·Put the top half aside and take a look at the bottom half. The bottom half is connected to accelerator grip by the accelerator cable.

4. ·The end of the accelerator wire sits in a groove and it is locked in place by means of a button, as shown in the picture. Slip the button out of the groove.

   ·Observe that, as you rotate the accelerator, the wire winds around in the groove and so it is pulled.

   ·When the accelerator wire is pulled, it sends more air-fuel mixture into the engine and hence the bike accelerates.

5. ·As you can see in the picture here, the accelerator cable is connected to the bottom half of the hub through a tube.

·You will be able to separate the cable and hub by rotating the tube shown by the arrow.

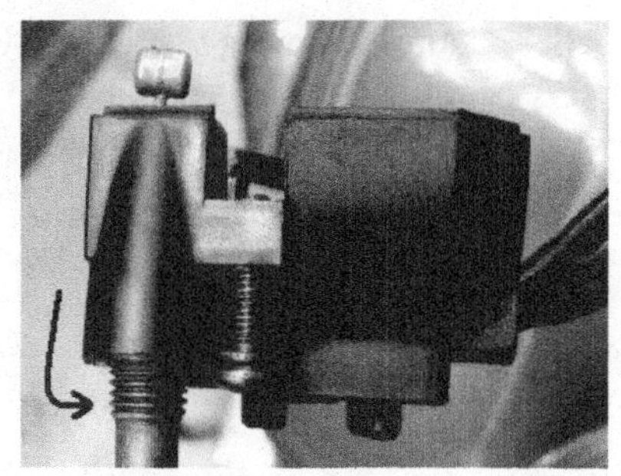

6. ·Once the cable comes out, it will look like this.

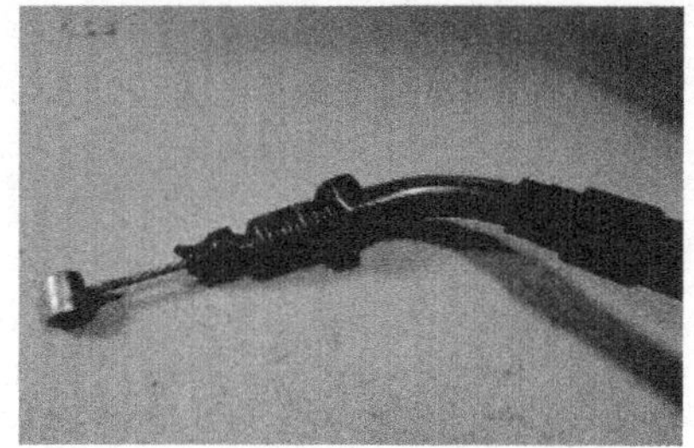

7. ·Now that you have successfully released the wire from the throttle grip end, let's proceed to the other end which is located at the carburettor.

·You will find a black box next to the engine like in the picture if you look from the kick rod side of your bike. This box is called throttle cable drum cover.

·Remove the two screws shown by the circles.

8. ·After removing the two screws you will be able to pull the cover out as shown in the picture.

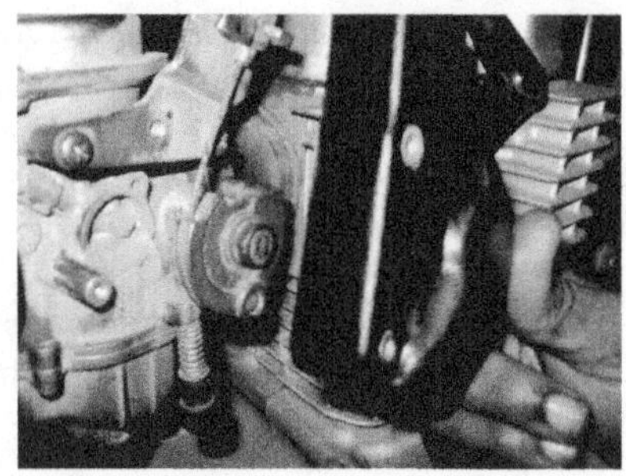

9. ·Inside, you will find a set-up like in the picture. There is a triangular disk to which the throttle wire is attached.

·The accelerator cable is connected to this by means of a button.

·Turn the accelerator and see what this disk does. You will note that it will turn as shown by the arrows.

·Also take a look at the two nuts shown in the circle.

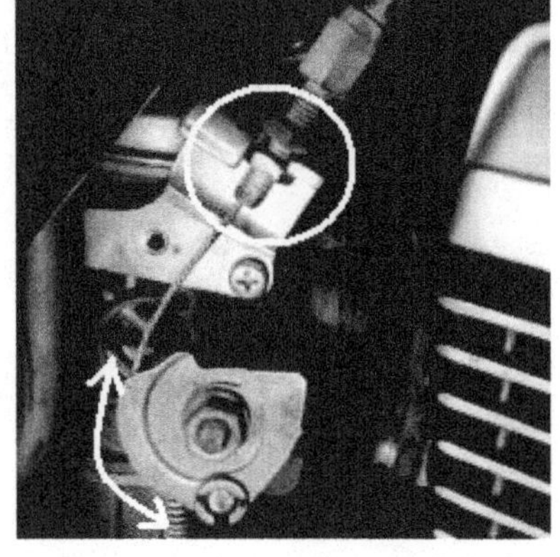

10. ·To remove the accelerator cable, loosen the top nut first as shown in the picture.

11. ·Then slide the cable out as
shown in the picture.

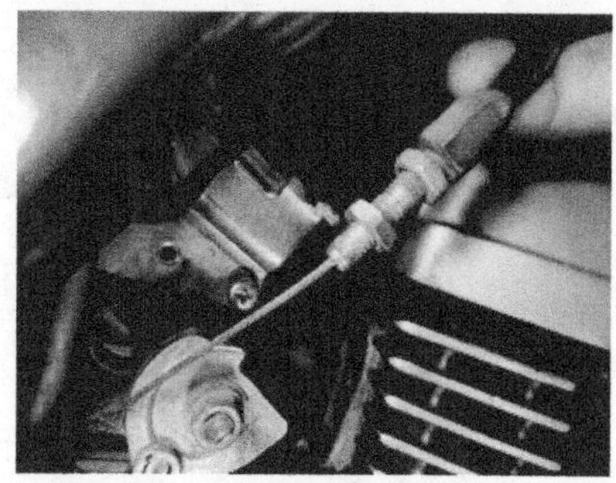

12. ·Then turn the plate clockwise
with your finger.

·Now, you can pull the button
out from the slot as shown in
the inset.

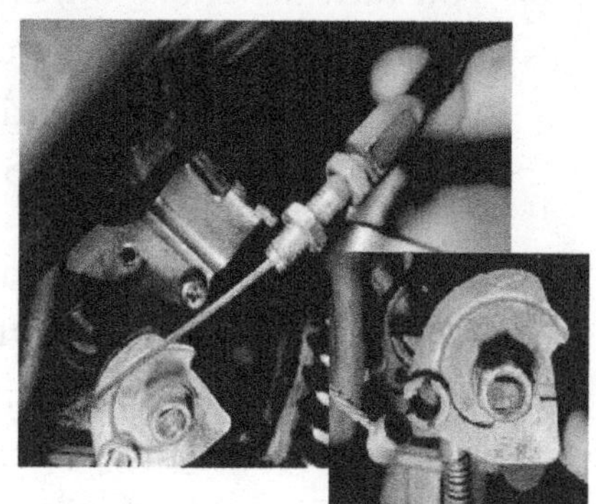

Now as you have successfully released the accelerator
cable at its both ends, you can simply pull it out.
Replacing it with a new one would be straightforward
as you know how to connect it at both ends.

Choke Cable

Spanner of size 14

Phillips screwdriver

The Choke cable is connected at two ends, one end at the choke lever (this is mostly called the choke, where you turn the choke on/off), and the other end to the carburettor. When you pull the choke lever, a small valve (called Starting Enrichment valve) allows more fuel into the engine to help it start easily.

Choke cables are mostly maintenance free and will last really long. But do check the movement and operation of the choke once in a while. If you do need to change the cable, follow these instructions.

1. ·Choke cable connects the choke knob to the carburettor.

    ·To remove the choke cable, you need to open the hub next to the choke knob pointed out by the box.

2. ·Look at the bottom of the hub to find 2 screws shown in the picture.

·Remove the two screws shown and open the hub.

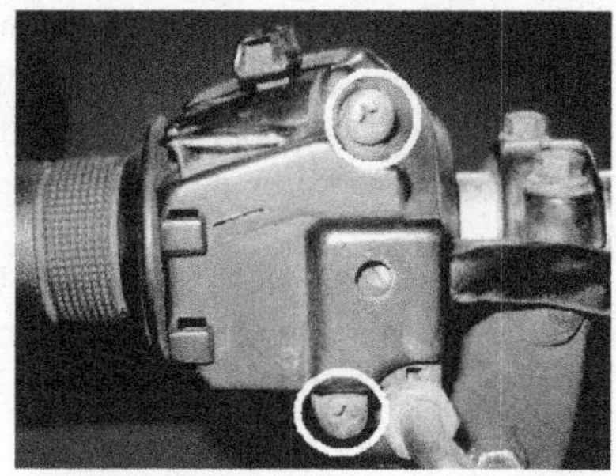

3. ·After removing the two screws, you will be able to separate the two halves as shown in the picture here.

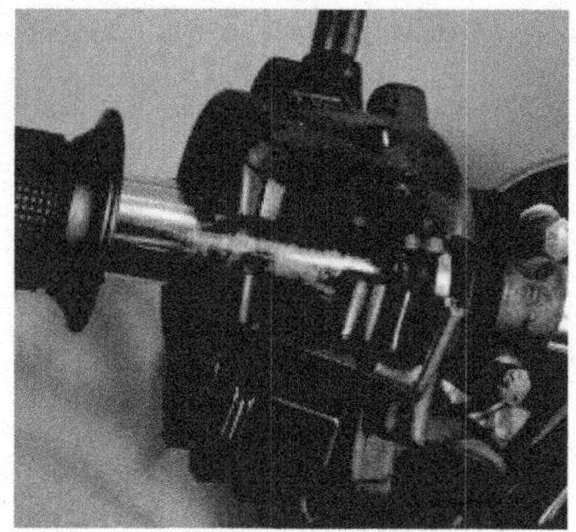

4. ·The choke cable is attached to the choke knob by means of a button as shown in the picture.

·To remove the cable, simply pull the button out.

·Now let's go the bottom end which is connected to the carburettor.

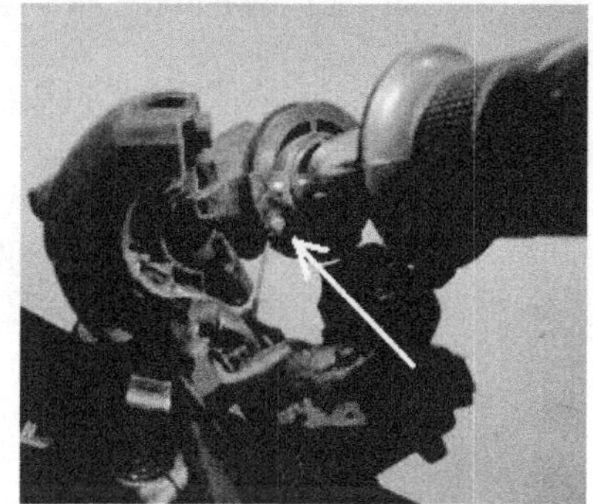

5. ·Take a look at the carburettor from the gear lever side. It is the metallic part highlighted by the box in the picture here.

·You will see that the carburettor is connected to 3 black tubes, **A**, **C** and **F** as shown in the picture.

·**A** is called the air vent hose

·**C** is the choke cable

·**F** is the fuel hose connecting the tank and the carburettor.

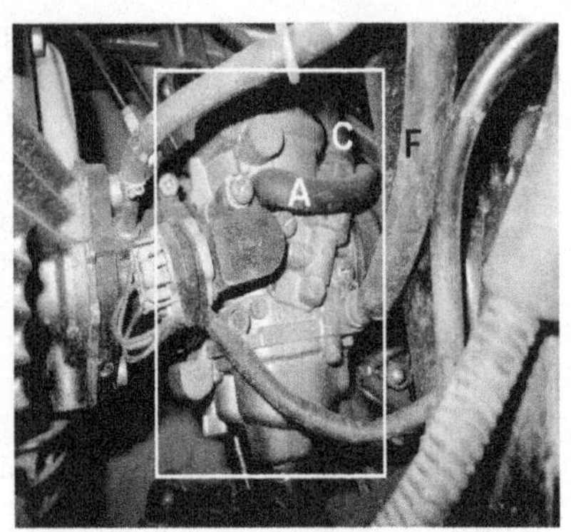

6. ·Because the choke cable is behind A, you need to remove **A** first.

·You can simply pull the tube out.

·Once you pull **A** out, you will be able to see and reach the Choke cable as shown in the picture.

7. ·Now you can remove the choke cable by simply unscrewing it out of the carburettor as shown by the arrow.

8. ·After you pull the choke cable out, you will note that, it looks like in the picture here.

·The cable is attached to a plug like thing with a spring. This is called the SE valve.

·When you pull the choke, this plug moves up and allows more petrol to mix in the air. This helps the engine to start easily.

The purpose of choke is simply to deliver more petrol into the engine. When the engine is cold, only a part of the fuel entering it will vaporise. So, extra fuel is needed to produce enough fuel (vapours) for combustion. Once the engine gets hot enough, most of the fuel will start to vaporise so we need to shut the choke. Leaving the choke on after the engine has got hot enough is very bad for your bike. Fuel gets wasted, excess carbon will be deposited in your engine and the performance and life of your engine will be affected. So every time you start your bike with the choke on, make sure you turn it off as soon as your bike is warmed up for a few seconds. Never drive while leaving choke in on position.

Speedometer cable

 Phillips screwdriver

Speedometer cable is connected at two ends. One end is connected underneath the speedometer dial; other end is connected to the hub at the front wheel. Inside the hub is a small gear. As the wheel rotates, the speedometer gear rotates and that in turn rotates the speedometer cable. And the other end of the cable is attached to the speedometer display.

If your speedometer isn't working, it's likely that the speedometer gear or the dial has a problem. The cable itself is mostly trouble free and doesn't need regular maintenance. If you have a problem with the speedometer, consult the service centre. If cable is the problem, you can change it very easily as shown below.

1. ·To remove the Speedometer cable, you need to remove the front cowl (dome) first. Refer to the Dome/Cowl removal chapter to learn how to do it.

   ·After removing the cowl/ dome, if you look under the speedometer dial, you will find a cable attached to it as shown in the picture.

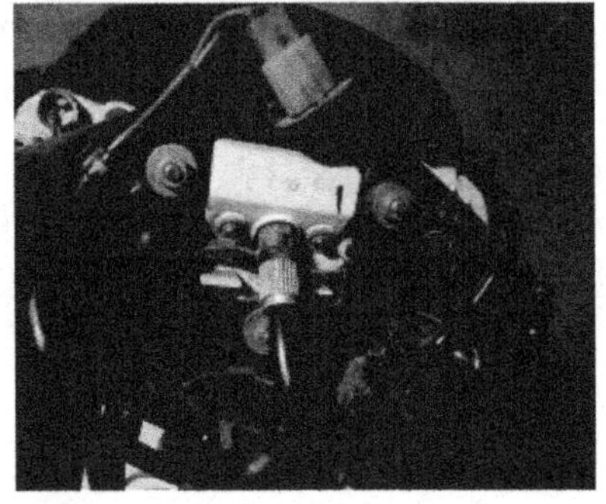

2. ·You can remove it by simply unscrewing the grooved tube shown above.

·Inside, you will find the speedometer cable as shown here.

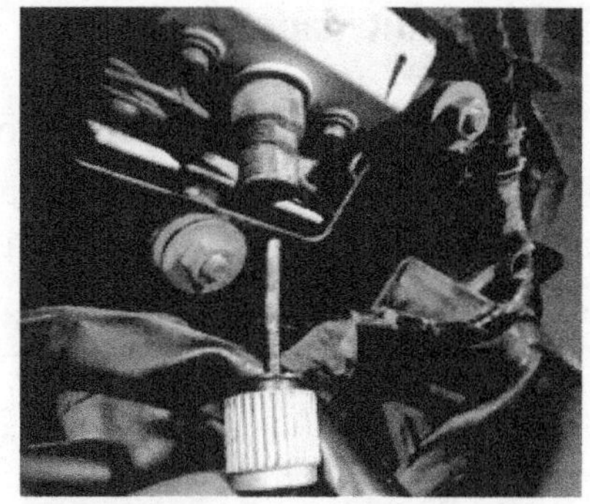

3. ·Now to remove it from the bottom end, take a look at the front wheel shown in the picture.

·You will find the other end of the Speedometer cable.

4. ·To disconnect the speedometer cable from this end, put a screwdriver in the slot given and push the cable outwards as shown in the picture.

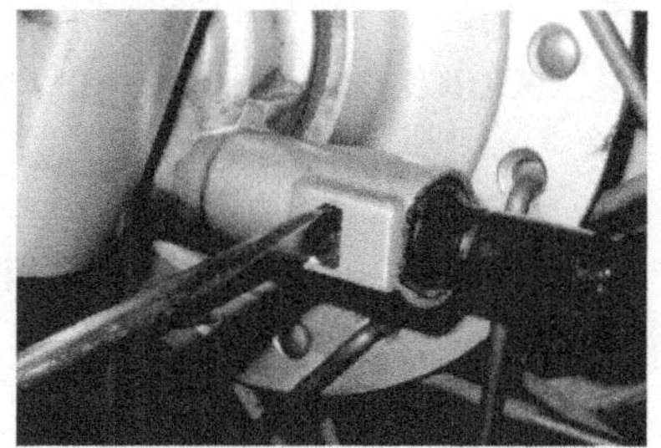

5. ·Once you get the cable out of the socket observe the end, it looks as shown in the picture.

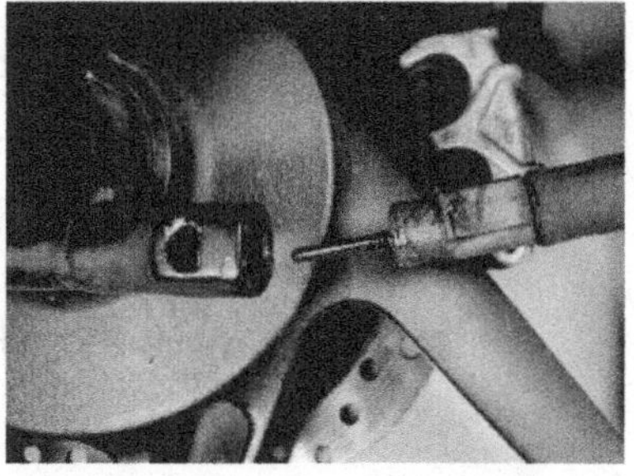

Maintenance

Because cables are made of a bunch of very thin strands of metal, they won't snap at once. The strands start breaking one by one and so, if you keep checking the cables periodically, you will be able to identify damage and replace them in time.

By checking the cables regularly by following the maintenance chart, you will be able to identify any wear in the cables, so that you can replace them in time by following the simple steps explained in this chapter.

Working on cables and adjusting the play is easy, but it's also a bit messy. So keep a rag handy and get started.

Clutch cable play adjustment

 Spanners of sizes 8,10

Adjusting play simply means loosening or tightening the cables to most of us. But clutch play is something quite different. If you try pulling the clutch lever slowly, you will observe that it moves freely over a little distance before you can actually feel the "spring action". Over this little distance, the clutch cable's movement doesn't actually do anything. The amount of this distance is called play.

If play is less, the clutch disengages as soon as you start pulling the lever; if it's more, the clutch won't disengage until the lever is pulled much further. Also, no play or little play will keep the cable under continuous tension which is obviously bad over a period of time. Periodic play adjustment is necessary to compensate for stretch in the cable and for gradual wear of the clutch friction plates, this can be adjusted to suit individual driving styles. However, the ideal play is 1-2cm.

Now let's see how to adjust the play.

As explained in the Clutch Cable chapter, the adjusting nut and lock nut are used to adjust clutch play.

First, loosen the lock nut.

Then, turn the adjusting nut to increase or decrease clutch play.

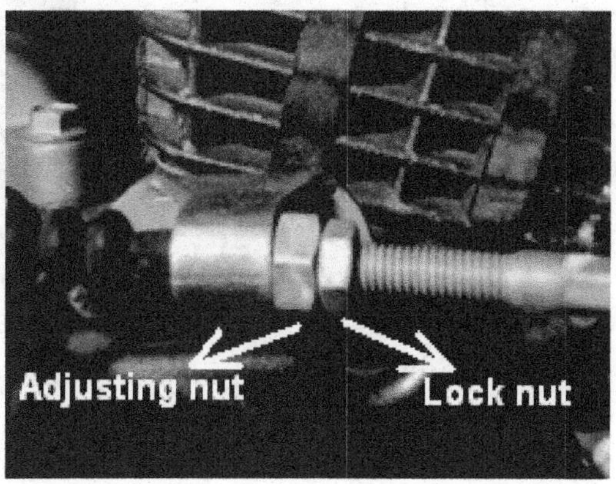

Once you have achieved the desired play of 10-20mm, hold the adjusting nut with one hand and tighten the lock nut.

Throttle/Accelerator cable play adjustment

Spanners of sizes 8 and 10

Phillips screwdriver

Just like the clutch cable, the accelerator/throttle cable needs some play. Ideally it should be between 2mm-6mm. Some play should be allowed so that the cable isn't under continuous tension. Throttle cable play can be adjusted at two locations; near the throttle grip and at the carburettor end.

To adjust play at the carburettor end, remove the throttle cable drum cover by following the instructions in Accelerator/Throttle Cable Removal section. Then, take a look at the two nuts shown in the picture (highlighted by the circle). The nut on top is lock nut and the bottom nut is the adjusting nut.

To adjust play, you need to loosen the lock nut and turn the adjusting nut while checking play. When the desired play is achieved, tighten the lock nut and then you are done.

For minor adjustments in throttle play, you don't need to go through all this. You can adjust at the throttle grip itself.

To do this, locate the adjusting mechanism as shown in the picture. Pull the dust cover off to access the adjuster and lock nuts as shown in the picture. Now, as usual, loosen the lock

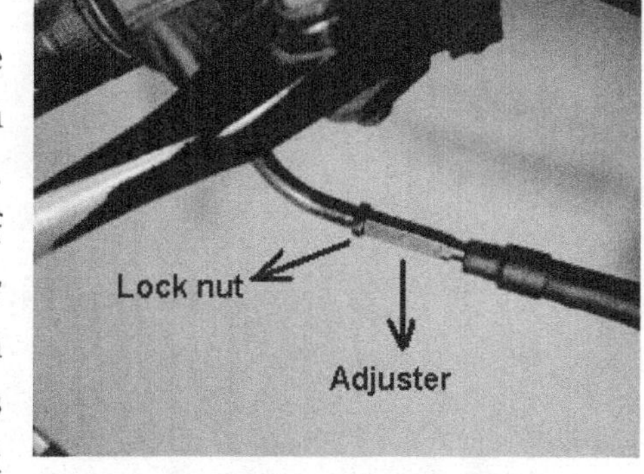

nut and turn the adjuster to achieve the desired play. Once you are done, tighten the lock nut and pull the dust cover back on.

Hoses/Pipes

 Pliers

Hoses or Pipes are used on your bike to transfer air, fuel, etc. from one place to another. These hoses can be classified into three categories: Fuel Hose, Air supply Hoses and Drain Hoses.

Fuel Hose

The fuel hose transfers fuel from the tank to the carburettor. It is connected to the Fuel On/Off valve on the tank and the other end is connected to the carburettor.

Fuel flows from the tank into a fuel strainer where impurities are filtered. It then flows through a strainer screen where it is further filtered. Then it flows through the hose into the carburettor.

Even after all this filtering business, the fuel pipe can sometimes get blocked especially when you park your bike for long periods of time. Also, the pipe will develop cracks sometimes which will result in fuel leaks. So, it is recommended to check the condition of the hose during every servicing schedule.

Air Supply Hoses

These hoses are used to pass air from one place to the other. They are located behind one of the side panels. Please refer to the Side Panels section to learn how to remove them. Once you gain access to the pipes, you can remove them by simply pulling them out.

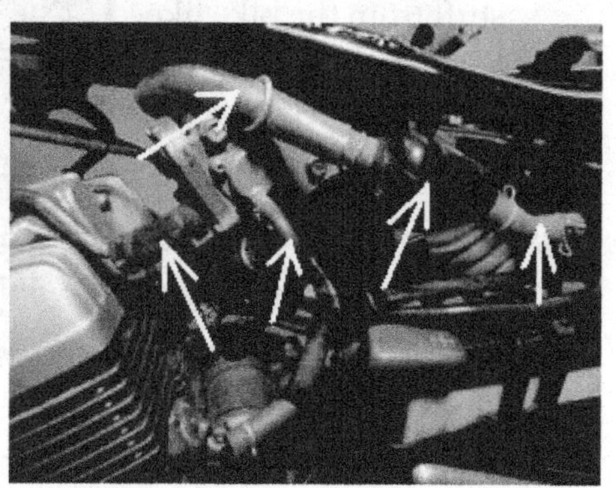

Check them for blocks, leaks or cracks.

Apart from these, there is another pipe called the crank case breather hose. To look at it you need to look from the kick rod side. It connects the air filter housing and crank case.

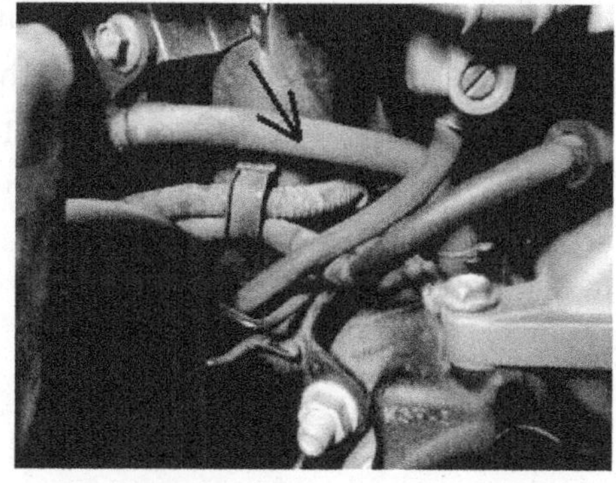

It might look confusing in the picture but you will spot it. This hose also needs regular inspection especially if you have driven in wet areas or when you have driven with full open throttle for long distances.

Drain Hoses

These hoses are used to drain off unwanted stuff from the bike like battery drain hose, carburettor drain hose and air filter housing drain hose etc. The battery drain hose drains off overflowing electrolyte and fumes. 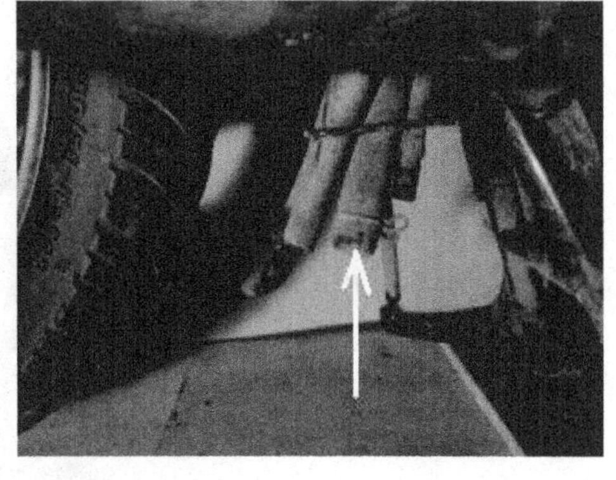 The electrolyte has acid in it and can eat away metal or anything for that matter. So make sure the drain hose is properly routed and is left to hang under the bike.

The carburettor drain hose drains off petrol from the float bowl when you loosen the drain screw. And the air filter housing drain hose drains off any solid particles that might have entered in to the housing. This hose has a cap at its end as pointed out in the picture. This cap needs to be emptied once in a while.

Maintenance

Maintenance of all hoses involves the same principle. You need to check them for cracks, loose connections and blocks. Usually the pipes crack where the metal hose clips are tightened. You also need to make sure they are routed without any drastic kinks which can block free flow.

Battery

The battery in your bike supplies the necessary electricity to run the starter motor when you try to start the engine. It also substitutes the alternator in providing electricity to different components like lights, indicators, horn, etc.

Battery is an electro-chemical device which uses chemical reaction to produce electricity. It consists of a series of positive and negative electrodes dipped in an electrolyte. The electrolyte is a solution of sulphuric acid and distilled water.

Removing/Refitting

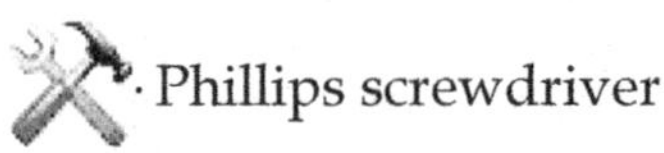 · Phillips screwdriver

 · Always wear gloves before handling your battery. In case you have to touch it, make sure you wash your hands well.

· Sulphuric acid in the battery is extremely dangerous if it gets in to your eyes. If it does, rinse your eyes in water for 5 minutes and visit a doctor.

· The acid is highly corrosive in nature and can cause burns on your skin, damage your clothes and metal surfaces.

· Batteries sometimes give out fumes which are flammable. So don't work near naked flames.

1. Your bike's battery is located behind one of your side panels (left panel for new model and right on the kick start model).

    Please refer to the Side Panel section to see how they can be removed.

    Once you find the battery, you will note that it is held in place by a metal brace as shown in the picture. To remove the brace, remove the screw from the point highlighted in the picture.

2. Now, open the brace as shown in the picture to access the battery.

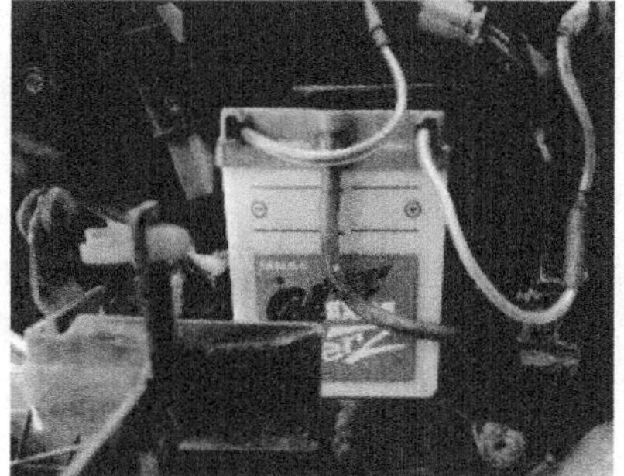

3. Next disconnect the cables and the drain pipe.

    It is important that you remember to remove the negative terminal first. Then remove the positive terminal. There are + and – signs on the battery to help you out.

    Then, pull the battery out of the bike.

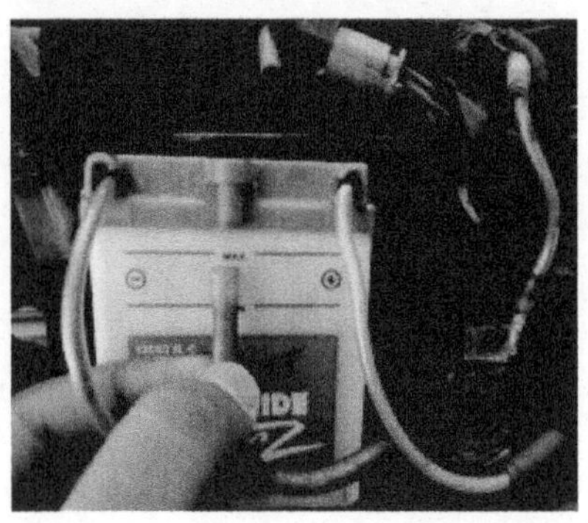

To refit the battery, simply follow the above steps in reverse order. But note that you have to connect the positive first and then the negative. Also, don't forget to connect the drain pipe properly.

Maintenance

 · Screwdriver

1. ·Look at the battery in the light. You will be able to see the electrolyte level.

    ·If it is between the MAX and MIN markings, the battery is fine.

    ·If the level is on or below MIN, you will have to top up your battery with distilled water.

    ·You can buy distilled water at most petrol stations.

2. ·To top up, you need to open the caps on top of the battery shown in the picture. But before you open them up, clean the surrounding area to prevent dirt from entering the cells.

·They might look different depending on the battery's make, but are quite obvious to find.

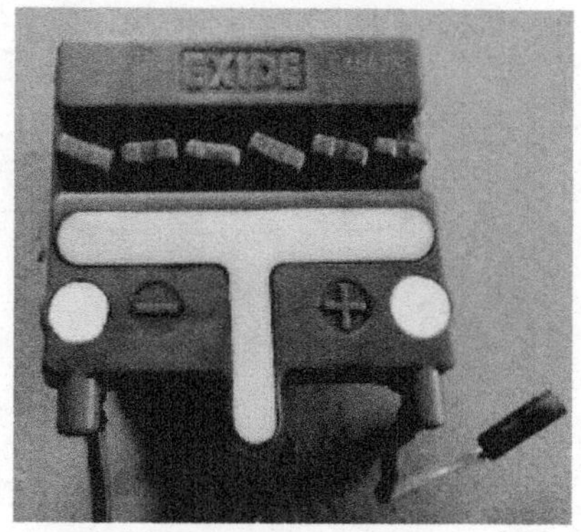

·To open them, simply pull them out in this case. If your battery has flat caps with provision for opening with screwdriver, use a screwdriver and unscrew them.

·Then slowly pour in the distilled water. Use a funnel if you have to.

·Remember that, your battery is not like a tub. It is made up of individual compartments (called cells). Each cell is sealed off by a cap (like the ones shown in the picture).

·So, when you pour distilled water into one cell, it won't flow into the others. You will have to top up each cell making sure the level is between MAX and MIN markings.

Miscellaneous

 Phillips screwdriver

Seat

Most of you might already know how to take your seat out, but to those who didn't bother to try; this is how you do it.

1. To remove the seat you need to unlock the seat lock near the left rear indicator.

   After unlocking, pull the small lever behind it and lift the seat simultaneously.

   Then simply lift the seat off your bike.

Side Panels

You will need to remove the side panels to perform several maintenance operations. Follow these instructions to see how it's done.

1. ·To open the side panel, first remove seat. Please refer to the Seat section to see how it's done.

   ·Then remove the three screws pointed out by the circles.

   ·Then by holding the side panel firmly, pull it towards you from points marked by the "+" signs.

   ·The side panel has two bosses at the points which sit in holes provided on the tank chassis.

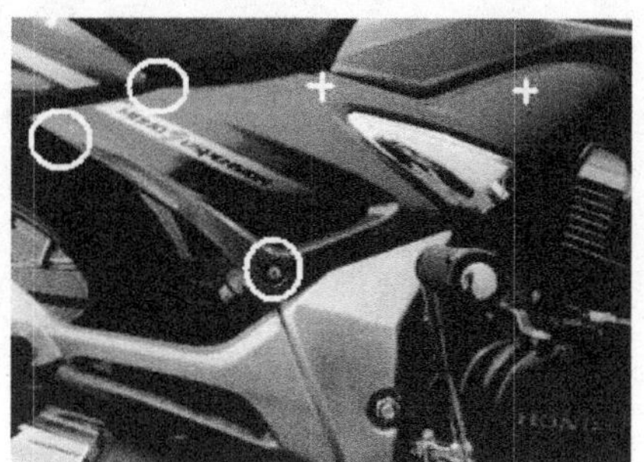

2. ·The picture here shows the bosses on the side panel.

   ·While refitting push these bosses into place first and then tighten the three screws.

Front dome/cowl

The Front Cowl generally referred to as, the Front Dome, houses the headlight, the windshield and the front turn signal lights (indicators). To replace any of these components, you need to remove the cowl. There is no maintenance involved with the cowl, but to access the speedometer cable you need to remove it.

1. ·For the first model Unicorn, to remove the font cowl (dome), remove the two screws highlighted in the picture using a Phillips (star) screwdriver.

2. ·For the new model Unicorn, you need remove the screw shown in the picture. There is a similar screw on the other side, remove that too.

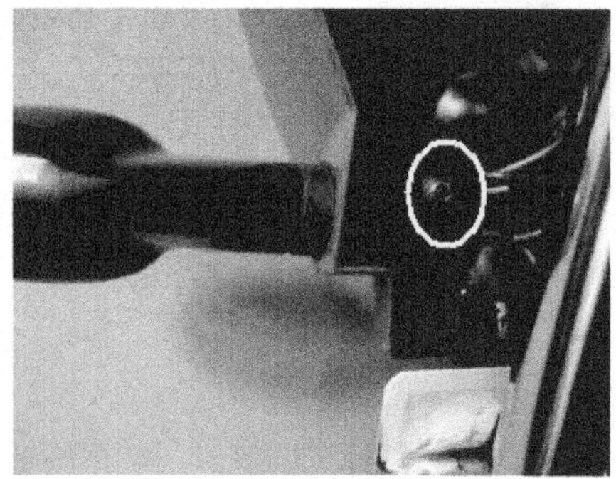

3. ·Now, you can pull the black cover(s) out as shown in the picture.

·Note that the cover has a boss on it. This fits into the hole on the dome as pointed out in the picture.

·Once you remove the covers, the rest is exactly same as the old model.

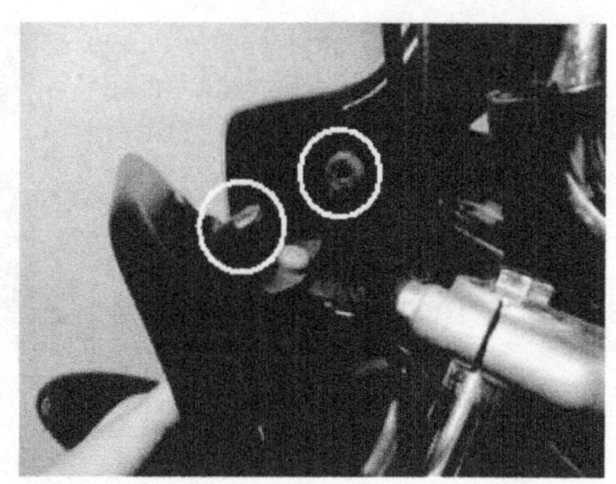

4. ·After removing the two screws shown above, come around to the front of your bike.

·When you are in front of your bike, remove the number plate from its frame using a screwdriver.

·Then, look at the number plate frame from the bottom, in the direction of the arrow.

5. ·You will find 3 screws as shown in the picture.

·The screw in the middle (pointed out by the circle) holds the cowl (dome) in place, and the two on its either side fix the number plate to the cowl (dome).

·Remove the middle screw using a screwdriver or a spanner.

6. ·Now, holding the cowl (dome) with both hands gently pull the bottom towards you (away from the bike).

·Then disengage the top and pull out the entire front cowl (dome) as shown in the picture.

·Make sure that you don't pull it very hard and far, because this cowl (dome) has a power supply cable attached to it, as shown in next step.

7. ·Once the Cowl (dome) comes into your hands, note that the power cables from the headlight and the indicators are connected to the bike's main wiring through a socket as shown in the picture.

8. ·Pull this plug out to disconnect the power cable as shown in the picture.

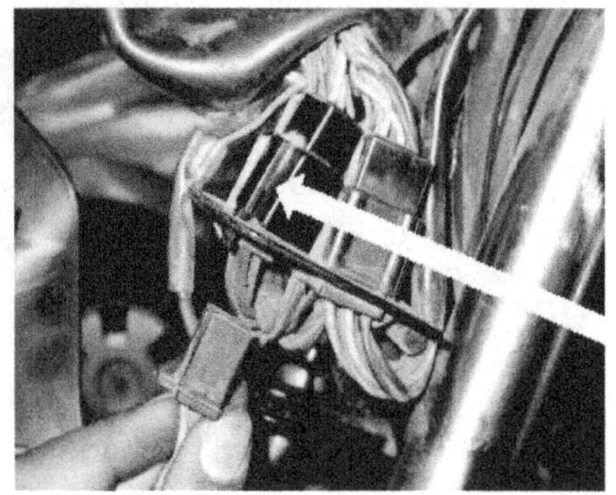

9. ·Once you pull the socket out, the front cowl (dome) can be separated from the bike.

·Place it gently on a piece of cloth so it won't get scratched.

10. ·To fix the cowl back on, connect the power supply cable first,

·Align the right side screw hole first (shown by the circle in the picture), and then align the bottom screw hole with your other hand. The cowl (dome) will automatically snap into the correct position.

·Before tightening the screws to fix the front cowl (dome), turn the ignition on and check if the bulbs are working fine.

Speedometer gear lubrication

Whenever you remove the wheel, it is advisable to lubricate the speedometer gear. To do so, please refer the front wheel removal

section to learn how to remove the speedometer gear box. The gear can be simply lifted out of the gearbox as shown in the picture. Apply grease liberally and refit it inside the gear box.

Suspension operation

It is important to check the suspension operation, both at the front and rear, periodically. Check for any oil leaks on the front. It is usually caused due to broken oil seals. Also, check if the operation is smooth. Sit on your bike with your feet on the floor, hold the front brake and push the handle to depress the front suspension. If it feels unusually hard or if you hear odd noises, visit a service centre and have it checked.

Check the rear suspension in a similar fashion for leaks and operation. IF the operation is smooth but the suspension is too hard or soft for your liking, you can adjust it by turning the adjuster shown in the picture. To 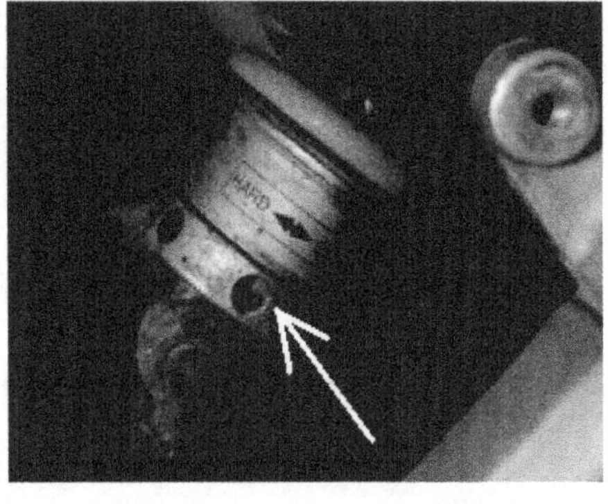 turn it, stick the small metal rod (also used to turn the spark plug wrench) in one of the slots and turn it. You could use a screwdriver or something similar also.

Faulty rear suspension cannot be repaired. They have to be replaced.

Setting the Engine's Idle Speed

Idle speed is the engines
speed (rpm) when
it is simply running
idly i.e. the speed of
the engine when in
neutral and when you
are not accelerating. It
is important to check
your engine's idle speed

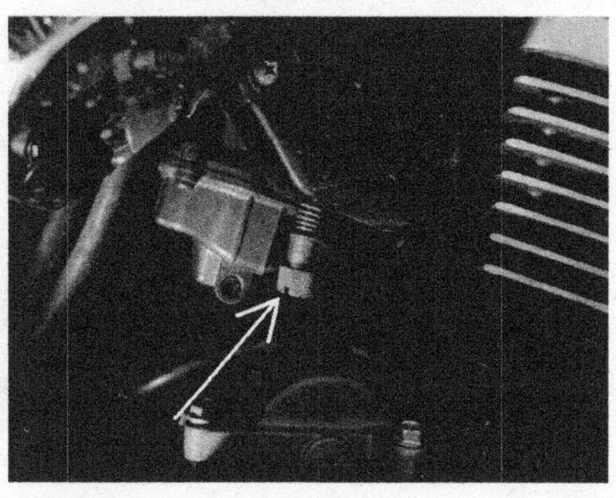

regularly because the engine spends a significant
period of time at this speed during day-to-day driving.

This speed should be just enough to keep the engine
running. If it's more than that, fuel will be simply
wasted.

The idle speed should be between **1300rpm-1500rpm.**

To set idle speed, you need to locate the idle adjustment
screw on the carburettor (shown in the picture). Start
the engine and while looking at the Tachometer (rpm
indicator), turn the idle adjusting screw and set the idle
speed to the right rpm.

Setting Headlight Aim

The direction and angle in which your headlight beam is projected has to be accurate to get maximum visibility at night. To do this, take a look at the front cowl (dome). If you look underneath the dome, 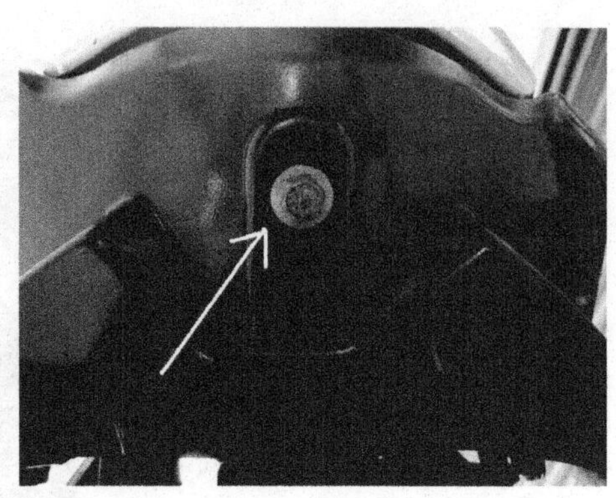 you will find a screw as shown in the picture. If you look closely, you will note that, near the screw there are markings on the cowl. To perfectly set the headlight aim, loosen this screw and then push/pull the headlight and make the screw align with the markings. Then tighten the screw again.

Few more words

Fuel efficiency

Fuel efficiency is what we worry about the most, but it is perhaps the least understood concept among many bikers. To get things straight, there isn't any MAGIC SCREW on your bike (or carburettor) that will drastically improve your bike's fuel efficiency. Especially the CV carburettor on your bike is not to be tinkered with. It is extremely difficult to re-tune if once faultily set.

Fuel efficiency is a result that depends on several complex things and we shall try to address the most important of them here. And hopefully, we will bust a few myths about fuel efficiency in the process.

Engine's rpm and Driving Style

Fuel efficiency is simply the amount of petrol your bike uses to travel a certain distance. The most important thing you need to remember in order to understand fuel efficiency is the engine's rpm. It is an indication of how fast your engine is running. And obviously, the faster it runs the more petrol it burns.

So, here is a little experiment for you to try. Next time you are driving keep an eye on the odometer. Just one eye though, the other needs to be on the road! Drive on a flat road at 40kmph in the highest possible gear (the engine shouldn't stall) and note the rpm. Now drive up a slope at the same speed and note the rpm. Do the same thing while you have a friend sitting on the back, when there is headwind, and while driving on a lower gear. You will note that the rpm will read higher in the above cases, which means you are burning more fuel.

Now, before you blame your friend or the uphill or the wind for wasting your fuel, think what the rpm reads when you are in an aggressive driving mood. Aggressive acceleration and braking burns a lot of fuel and also stresses your engine. Accelerating with as little rpm rise as possible will give you the best fuel economy and so does riding in the highest possible gear.

So in conclusion, proper driving style can save you a lot of fuel. Here are a few points to remember:

Accelerate smoothly

When you need to slow down, close the throttle completely first and make use of engine braking.

Shift your gears at the right rpm.

Drive in the highest gear possible.

Are you wondering how much difference does it make? There are several tests that suggest a 10% to 30% increase in fuel efficiency by simply driving less aggressively and making proper gear shifts.

Idling

When you are idling, you are simply burning fuel to stay where you are. So, whenever you need to wait for more than 1 minute – like at traffic signals, turn the engine off. If it's less than that, don't bother because your engine will burn more fuel to start, than to idle.

Also, if you are constantly turning the throttle slightly to keep the engine running at idle, you need to stop this practice. Your engine wants to stop because the idle speed is not properly set, or there is a problem at the carburettor or the air supply is bad. The first thing you need to do is to set the idle speed to 1300-1500 rpm. If your engine doesn't keep running, you need to visit a service centre.

The clutch mystery

There is a strange belief that using the clutch will burn more fuel. Clutch on its own has nothing to do with burning fuel. All your clutch does is it connects/disconnects your engine and transmission.

But, when you press the clutch lever while accelerating (or just holding the throttle fixed), you are wasting fuel. Think of it this way. Every time you are turning the throttle (even the slightest bit) while pressing the clutch lever, you are wasting fuel. That's the simple logic. So, when the throttle is closed, press the clutch lever to your heart's content, it won't affect your bike's fuel efficiency.

The other question many bikers have is whether or not it is okay to coast. Coasting is, to go down a slope or simply drive along with your clutch lever pressed without turning the accelerator/throttle. By doing this, your bike's engine will be idling and the bike will simply be rolling forward due to momentum. The answer depends on where you wish to coast. If it is an open road or a gentle slope with no possible hazards, it's perfectly alright as long as you are not in neutral. Never coast in neutral because, it is not uncommon in our country to find cattle or kids darting across the road unannounced. And if you are in gear, at least when you leave the clutch and press the brake, your bike will stop within a short distance.

But note that when you are done with coasting and wish to engage the clutch, due to the difference in speed the clutch plates will take a shock and can wear off faster.

Tyre Pressure

Tyre pressure is very important for fuel efficiency. Under-inflated tyres need more power to keep them rolling. So check tyre pressure frequently or every time you get fuel.

Maintaining right tyre pressure can improve your fuel efficiency up to 3%.

Air Filter

Air filters trap dust and other particles from the air before it's sent into the engine. But as this dust builds up, the amount of air that can pass through the air filter decreases. And when it gets too dirty, the amount of air that passes through it drastically decreases and your engine will start sucking in more fuel instead. This fuel remains partially unburnt and hence it is simply wasted. So, clean the air filter regularly. If your bike has a viscous air filter, replace it regularly. (Please refer to the Air Filter chapter to learn how to clean/replace and when to replace filters)

This can influence your fuel efficiency up to 10%.

Spark Plug

A faulty or dirty (fouled) plug can also severely affect your bike's fuel efficiency. A fouled plug won't fire up at the right time thus wasting fuel. Check spark plugs regularly and clean them. Please see the Spark Plug chapter to learn more.

Overall condition

Properly lubricated parts and a well maintained engine and carburettor will help a lot in improving your bike's fuel efficiency. So, if you take care of your bike properly by following a maintenance schedule, it will take care of your fuel expenses.

Modifications

Modifying your bike has to be just as scientific and valid from an engineering point of view as is the bike's actual design. Modifications are good as they get the maximum out of your bike's existing configuration, but how and what to modify involves careful study and analysis. The scope of modifications that can be made on motorcycles and their impact on performance will need a book on its own. We shall try to address the effect of some of these modifications on fuel economy.

Big tyres especially in the rear are a popular choice. Changing manufacturer's tyres is not recommended for both safety and from the fuel economy point of view. Big tyres are heavy and hence need more petrol to keep them rolling. They might look safe but they affect the overall weight distribution and balance of the bike.

Exhaust modifications are also a bad idea. Companies spend large amounts of money to find the most optimum exhaust system for your bike's configuration before they fit them on your bike. So changing an exhaust for better sound will almost certainly affect your bike's engine and fuel economy.

Crash guards are not mandatory! Yes it might sound crazy but they are not mandatory by law because how well they protect your legs in the event of a crash is a huge debate worldwide. But they do save your legs and the bike from scratches in case of a low speed crash. So, leaving on the crash guard that came with the bike is a good idea. Don't bother buying those huge crash guards that look like elephant tusks. They add too much weight and in fact can damage your frame in the event of a crash.

The best idea hence, is to leave the bike alone if its fuel efficiency that you want. But if you want to add a bit of "oomph", let your imagination run wild. But please keep safety in mind.

BEING A GOOD BIKER

In popular culture and in real life, we bikers have a notorious reputation that parallels the Kamikaze pilots of WW2. Though most of us are sober drivers mostly, there are times when we do terrorise fellow motorists and pedestrians. All it takes for that shift into road rage is a traffic jam or a fellow motorist or maybe even a bad movie. But please try your best to remind yourself the following while driving:

Drive considerately. Give way to others instead of edging in through the slightest possible gaps.

Don't leave your headlight in "HIGH BEAM" all the time. You should only use it to indicate PASS and when there is no oncoming traffic. Some riders seem to have a misconception that high beam gives better visibility. This is preposterous. It is no excuse blinding others by shining a high intensity light into their unsuspecting eyes. If visibility is bad in low beam, it means there is something wrong either with the lights (or your eyes). Get the headlight aim checked at a service centre.

Use those rear view mirrors. No. They don't bang into others while driving so stop worrying about it. Use them while overtaking and taking turns.

Stop honking unnecessarily. Some people seem to think that by blowing their horns madly they can make everybody else on the road disappear. Even at traffic signals, these people won't spare us. We are sure you are not one of them. But if you encounter someone like this, please don't bother enlightening them. Because they have most probably deafened themselves already.

Acknowledgement

Our wholehearted thanks to all the people who believed and supported the idea behind this book. We owe our gratitude to our friends Naveen, Gnan, Ravi, Kranthi, S.V. Reddy, Siraz and of course our families for their continuous help, feedback and support. And we thank Honda for making such a wonderfully designed motorcycle.

Made in the USA
Monee, IL
07 July 2026

56552391R00104